Kaplan Publishing are constantly finding new ways to make a difference to your studies and our exciting online resources really do offer something different to students looking for exam success.

This book comes with free MyKaplan online resources so that you can study anytime, anywhere. **This free online resource is not sold separately and is included in the price of the book.**

Having purchased this book, you have access to the following online study materials:

CONTENT	AAT	
	Text	Kit
Electronic version of the book	✓	✓
Progress tests with instant answers	✓	
Mock assessments online	✓	✓
Material updates	✓	✓

How to access your online resources

Kaplan Financial students will already have a MyKaplan account and these extra resources will be available to you online. You do not need to register again, as this process was completed when you enrolled. If you are having problems accessing online materials, please ask your course administrator.

If you are not studying with Kaplan and did not purchase your book via a Kaplan website, to unlock your extra online resources please go to www.mykaplan.co.uk/addabook (even if you have set up an account and registered books previously). You will then need to enter the ISBN number (on the title page and back cover) and the unique pass key number contained in the scratch panel below to gain access. You will also be required to enter additional information during this process to set up or confirm your account details.

If you purchased through Kaplan Flexible Learning or via the Kaplan Publishing website you will automatically receive an e-mail invitation to MyKaplan. Please register your details using this email to gain access to your content. If you do not receive the e-mail or book content, please contact Kaplan Publishing.

Your Code and Information

This code can only be used once for the registration of one book online. This registration and your online content will expire when the final sittings for the examinations covered by this book have taken place. Please allow one hour from the time you submit your book details for us to process your request.

Please scratch the film to access your MyKaplan code.

Please be aware that this code is case-sensitive and you will need to include the dashes within the passcode, but not when entering the ISBN. For further technical support, please visit www.MyKaplan.co.uk

AAT

AQ2016

External Auditing

EXAM KIT

This Exam Kit supports study for the following AAT qualifications:

AAT Professional Diploma in Accounting – Level 4

AAT Level 4 Diploma in Business Skills

AAT Professional Diploma in Accounting at SCQF Level 8

PUBLISHING

British Library Cataloguing-in-Publication Data

A catalogue record for this book is available from the British Library.

Published by:

Kaplan Publishing UK

Unit 2 The Business Centre

Molly Millar's Lane

Wokingham

Berkshire

RG41 2QZ

ISBN: 978-1-78740-296-6

Printed and bound in Great Britain.

CONTENTS

	Page
Unit-specific information	P.4
Index to questions and answers	P.5
Exam technique	P.9
Kaplan's recommended revision approach	P.10

Practice questions	1
Answers to practice questions	35
Mock assessment questions	63
Mock assessment answers	75

Features in this exam kit

In addition to providing a wide ranging bank of real exam style questions, we have also included in this kit:

- unit-specific information and advice on exam technique

- our recommended approach to make your revision for this particular unit as effective as possible.

You will find a wealth of other resources to help you with your studies on the AAT website:

www.aat.org.uk/

Quality and accuracy are of the utmost importance to us so if you spot an error in any of our products, please send an email to mykaplanreporting@kaplan.com with full details, or follow the link to the feedback form in MyKaplan.

Our Quality Co-ordinator will work with our technical team to verify the error and take action to ensure it is corrected in future editions.

UNIT-SPECIFIC INFORMATION

THE EXAM

FORMAT OF THE ASSESSMENT

The assessment will comprise twenty-three independent tasks. Students will be assessed by computer-based assessment.

In any one assessment, students may not be assessed on all content, or on the full depth or breadth of a piece of content. The content assessed may change over time to ensure validity of assessment, but all assessment criteria will be tested over time.

The learning outcomes for this unit are as follows:

	Learning outcome	Weighting
1	Demonstrate an understanding of the principles of auditing	5%
2	Demonstrate the importance of professional ethics	12%
3	Evaluate the audited entity's system of internal control	15%
4	Evaluate audit procedures for obtaining audit evidence	15%
5	Evaluate the planning process	33%
6	Evaluate audit procedures	20%
	Total	100%

Time allowed

2 hours

PASS MARK

The pass mark for all AAT CBAs is 70%.

 Always keep your eye on the clock and make sure you attempt all questions!

DETAILED SYLLABUS

The detailed syllabus and study guide written by the AAT can be found at:

www.aat.org.uk/

INDEX TO QUESTIONS AND ANSWERS

		Page Number	
		Question	**Answer**
LEVEL OF ASSURANCE			
1	Complete the statement	1	35
2	True or false	1	35
3	Level of assurance	1	35
LEGAL AND REGULATORY ISSUES			
4	True or false 1	2	35
5	True or false 2	2	36
6	Complete the statement 1	2	36
7	Complete the statement 2	2	36
8	True or false 3	3	36
9	True or false 4	3	36
10	International Auditing and Assurance Board 1	3	36
11	International Auditing and Assurance Board 2	3	36
EXTERNAL AUDITOR'S LIABILITY			
12	True or false 1	4	37
13	True or false 2	4	37
14	True or false 3	4	37
15	True or false 4	4	37
16	Complete the statement	4	37
ETHICAL ISSUES			
17	Ethical concepts	5	38
18	Familiarity	5	38
19	Jesse	5	38
20	Cayman	5	38
21	Identify the threats	6	38
SAFEGUARDS			
22	True or false 1	6	38
23	True or false 2	6	39
CONFIDENTIALITY			
24	Disclosure of information 1	7	39
25	Disclosure of information 2	7	39
26	Audit Junior	8	39
27	Weed	8	39

		Page Number	
		Question	**Answer**
INTERNAL CONTROL ENVIRONMENT			
28	Identify terms 1	8	40
29	Identify terms 2	9	40
CONTROL OBJECTIVES, RISKS AND PROCEDURES			
30	Select the appropriate term 1	9	40
31	Select the appropriate term 2	9	40
32	Select the appropriate term 3	10	41
33	Select the appropriate term 4	10	41
ACCOUNTING SYSTEMS			
34	Brown	10	41
35	Green	11	41
36	Morley	11	42
37	Nanny Plum	11	42
38	Wilson	12	42
39	Tages	12	43
40	Lemon Limes	12	43
RISKS AND CONTROLS			
41	Internal control procedures 1	13	43
42	Internal control procedures 2	13	43
43	Internal control procedures 3	13	43
44	Internal control procedures 4	14	43
45	Internal control procedures 5	14	43
VERIFICATION TECHNIQUES			
46	Identify procedures	14	44
47	Sales and receivables	15	44
48	Purchases 1	15	44
49	Purchases 2	15	44
50	Purchases 3	16	45
COMPUTER-ASSISTED AUDIT TECHNIQUES			
51	Test data and audit software 1	16	45
52	Test data and audit software 2	16	45
53	Test data and audit software 3	17	45
54	Test data and audit software 4	17	46
55	Test data and audit software 5	17	46

		Page Number	
		Question	*Answer*
SAMPLING			
56	Technical terms	18	46
57	Tests of detail	18	46
TESTS OF CONTROL AND SUBSTANTIVE PROCEDURES			
58	Audit approach 1	18	47
59	Audit approach 2	19	47
60	Test of control or substantive procedure 1	19	47
61	Test of control or substantive procedure 2	19	48
62	Test of control or substantive procedure 3	20	48
ACCOUNT BALANCES AND ASSOCIATED RISKS			
63	Analytical procedures 1	20	48
64	Analytical procedures 2	20	48
AUDIT RISK			
65	Components of audit risk	21	49
66	Audit risk statements	21	49
67	Control risk	21	49
68	Internal controls	22	49
69	True or false	22	49
70	Planning an audit	22	50
MATERIALITY			
71	True or false 1	23	50
72	True or false 2	23	50
73	True or false 3	23	50
74	True or false 4	23	51
75	True or false 5	23	51
76	True or false 6	24	51
77	True or false 7	24	51
INFORMATION AND RECOMMENDATIONS FOR THE AUDIT PLAN			
78	Top Notch	24	51
79	Florida Air Conditioning	24	52
80	Green	25	52
81	Pepco	25	53
82	Tileclose	25	53

		Page Number	
		Question	**Answer**
VERIFICATION OF ITEMS IN THE FINANCIAL STATEMENTS			
83	Smart Sense	25	53
84	Short Circuit	26	54
85	Honeysuckle	26	54
AUDIT DOCUMENTATION			
86	Purpose of working papers	26	55
87	Working papers 1	26	55
88	Working papers 2	27	55
89	Working papers 3	27	56
90	Working papers 4	27	56
91	Working papers 5	27	56
IDENTIFY MATTERS OF AN UNUSUAL NATURE			
92	Beach	28	56
93	Sunshine	28	56
94	Prep	28	56
95	Dodge	28	56
96	Sike	29	57
97	Trike	29	57
98	Jemima	29	57
99	Perch	29	57
DRAFT REPORTS AND RECOMMENDATIONS			
100	Pump	30	57
101	Delta	30	58
102	Pharo	30	58
AUDIT REPORTS			
103	Two companies	31	59
104	Wand	32	59
105	Ash & Medlar	32	60
106	Santa & Elves	32	60
107	Alba Co.	33	61

MOCK ASSESSMENT		
Questions and answers	63	75

KAPLAN PUBLISHING

EXAM TECHNIQUE

- **Do not skip any of the material** in the syllabus.

- **Read each question** *very* carefully.

- **Double-check your answer** before committing yourself to it.

- Answer **every** question – if you do not know an answer to a multiple choice question or true/false question, you don't lose anything by guessing. Think carefully before you **guess**.

- If you are answering a multiple-choice question, **eliminate first those answers that you know are wrong.** Then choose the most appropriate answer from those that are left.

- **Don't panic** if you realise you've answered a question incorrectly. Getting one question wrong will not mean the difference between passing and failing.

Computer-based exams – tips

- Do not attempt a CBA until you have **completed all study material** relating to it.

- On the AAT website there is a CBA demonstration. It is **ESSENTIAL** that you attempt this before your real CBA. You will become familiar with how to move around the CBA screens and the way that questions are formatted, increasing your confidence and speed in the actual exam.

- Be sure you understand how to use the **software** before you start the exam. If in doubt, ask the assessment centre staff to explain it to you.

- Questions are **displayed on the screen** and answers are entered using keyboard and mouse. At the end of the exam, you are given a certificate showing the result you have achieved.

- In addition to the traditional multiple-choice question type, CBAs will also contain **other types of questions**, such as number entry questions, drag and drop, true/false, pick lists or drop down menus or hybrids of these.

- In some CBAs you will have to type in complete computations or written answers.

- You need to be sure you **know how to answer questions** of this type before you sit the exam, through practice.

KAPLAN'S RECOMMENDED REVISION APPROACH

QUESTION PRACTICE IS THE KEY TO SUCCESS

Success in professional examinations relies upon you acquiring a firm grasp of the required knowledge at the tuition phase. In order to be able to do the questions, knowledge is essential.

However, the difference between success and failure often hinges on your exam technique on the day and making the most of the revision phase of your studies.

The **Kaplan Study Text** is the starting point, designed to provide the underpinning knowledge to tackle all questions. However, in the revision phase, poring over text books is not the answer.

Kaplan Pocket Notes are designed to help you quickly revise a topic area; however you then need to practise questions. There is a need to progress to exam style questions as soon as possible, and to tie your exam technique and technical knowledge together.

The importance of question practice cannot be over-emphasised.

The recommended approach below is designed by expert tutors in the field, in conjunction with their knowledge of the examiner and the specimen assessment.

You need to practise as many questions as possible in the time you have left.

OUR AIM

Our aim is to get you to the stage where you can attempt exam questions confidently, to time, in a closed book environment, with no supplementary help (i.e. to simulate the real examination experience).

Practising your exam technique is also vitally important for you to assess your progress and identify areas of weakness that may need more attention in the final run up to the examination.

In order to achieve this we recognise that initially you may feel the need to practice some questions with open book help.

Good exam technique is vital.

KAPLAN PUBLISHING

THE KAPLAN REVISION PLAN

Stage 1: Assess areas of strengths and weaknesses

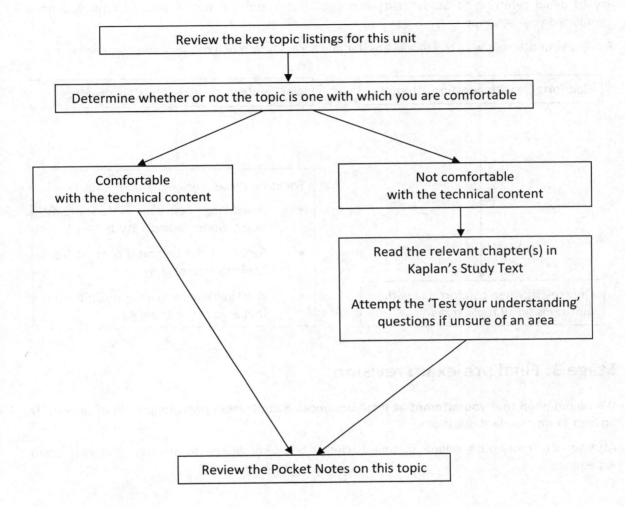

Review the key topic listings for this unit

Determine whether or not the topic is one with which you are comfortable

Comfortable
with the technical content

Not comfortable
with the technical content

Read the relevant chapter(s) in
Kaplan's Study Text

Attempt the 'Test your understanding'
questions if unsure of an area

Review the Pocket Notes on this topic

Stage 2: Practice questions

Follow the order of revision of topics as presented in this Kit and attempt the questions in the order suggested.

Try to avoid referring to Study Texts and your notes and the model answer until you have completed your attempt.

Review your attempt with the model answer and assess how much of the answer you achieved.

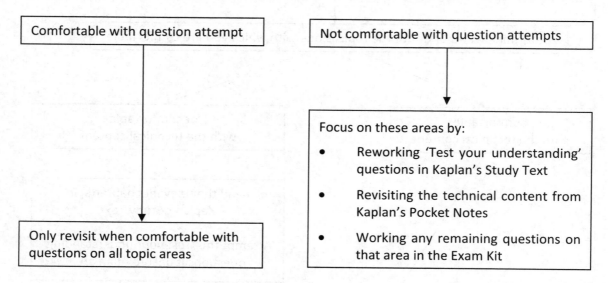

Comfortable with question attempt	Not comfortable with question attempts

Focus on these areas by:

- Reworking 'Test your understanding' questions in Kaplan's Study Text

- Revisiting the technical content from Kaplan's Pocket Notes

- Working any remaining questions on that area in the Exam Kit

Only revisit when comfortable with questions on all topic areas

Stage 3: Final pre-exam revision

We recommend that you **attempt at least one mock examination** containing a set of previously unseen exam-standard questions.

Attempt the mock CBA online in timed, closed book conditions to simulate the real exam experience.

Section 1

PRACTICE QUESTIONS

LEVEL OF ASSURANCE

1   Complete the statement below on the overall objectives of the external auditor in conducting an audit of financial statements by filling in the gaps:

The overall objectives of the external auditor are to obtain _____ assurance about whether the financial statements are free from _____ misstatement, whether due to fraud or error, thereby enabling the auditor to _____ on whether the financial statements are prepared in all material respects in accordance with _____ .

Select from: absolute, all, an applicable financial reporting framework, express an opinion, International Standards on Auditing, material, provide a guarantee, reasonable.

2   Tick the appropriate box for each of the following statements:

	True	False
(a) Auditors aim to give absolute assurance over the accuracy of the financial statements.		
(b) An audit includes examining, on a test basis, evidence supporting the amounts and disclosures in the financial statements.		

3   Identify the level of assurance provided by the following extract from an auditor's report:

In our opinion, the financial statements give a true and fair view of the state of the company's affairs as at 31 December 20X4 and of its profit for the year then ended.

Reasonable assurance	Limited assurance

LEGAL AND REGULATORY ISSUES

4   **Select whether the following statements are true or false in respect of professional scepticism.**

	True	False
(a) The auditor must maintain professional scepticism throughout the duration of the audit.		
(b) The client must maintain their professional scepticism throughout the duration of the audit.		

5   **Select whether the following statements are true or false in respect of professional scepticism.**

	True	False
(a) Professional scepticism refers to the auditor not believing anything the client says to them.		
(b) Professional scepticism refers to the questioning mind the auditor should maintain.		

6   **Complete the following statement on the respective responsibilities of the external auditor and management in conducting an audit of financial statements, by filling in the gaps using drag and drop.**

It is the responsibility of the _____ to prepare the annual financial statements for the company and it is the responsibility of the _____ to report to _____ whether in their opinion the financial statements show a _____.

Select from: Company Accountant, Correct set of accounts, Directors, External Auditors, Finance Director, Internal Auditor, Shareholders, True and Fair view

7   **Complete the following statement on the key attributes required of the external auditor.**

The most important professional attribute of an auditor is their _____. This enables the auditor to _____ as to the truth and fairness of the financial statements to the shareholders and gives assurance as to the _____ of the auditor.

Select from: Independence, Objectivity, Inexperience, Reputation, Express an opinion, True and Fair view, Training needs, Experience.

8 **Tick the appropriate box for each of the following statements:**

	True	False
(a) The auditors are responsible for preparing the financial statements on which they report.		
(b) The amounts in the financial statements are stated precisely.		
(c) The external auditor provides reasonable assurance on the future viability of the audited entity.		

9 **Tick the appropriate box for each of the following statements:**

	True	False
(a) The IAASB works to improve the uniformity of auditing practices exclusively in the UK.		
(b) The IAASB's standards contain basic principles and essential procedures together with related guidance in the form of explanatory and other material, including appendices.		

10 **Which one of the following statements best describes the role of the International Auditing and Assurance Board (IAASB)?**

The IAASB is responsible for:

A   setting auditing standards which are compulsory throughout the world.

B   monitoring auditors to ensure that they comply with auditing standards.

C   investigating and disciplining auditors who fail to comply with auditing standards.

D   setting auditing standards which facilitate the convergence of national and international auditing standards.

11 **Which one of the following statements best describes the authority of International Standards on Auditing (ISAs) issued by the International Auditing and Assurance Board (IAASB)?**

A   ISAs are best practice and can be followed by the auditor if they wish.

B   ISAs are standards that compete with local standards and the auditor can choose which to use.

C   ISAs are mandatory on all audits undertaken in the countries which have adopted ISAs unless the auditor has good reason for non-compliance.

D   ISAs must be followed at all times and take precedence over Company Law of an individual country.

EXTERNAL AUDITOR'S LIABILITY

12 Tick the appropriate box for each of the following statements:

		True	False
(a)	The primary duty of an auditor as set out in s235 of the Companies Act 2006 requires him to report to the company's members on every set of accounts requiring statutory audit.		
(b)	The external auditor has a statutory duty to detect fraud as part of the main duties of the audit.		

13 Tick the appropriate box for each of the following statements:

		True	False
(a)	The external auditor has a common law duty of care towards certain third parties under the law of tort.		
(b)	The external auditor has a duty to exercise 'reasonable skill and care' to the client and any breach may lead to a claim of negligence by the client.		

14 Tick the appropriate box for each of the following statements:

		True	False
(a)	Professional Indemnity Insurance is compulsory for all members of the Institute who have a practising certificate and are engaged in public practice, regardless of the amount of practice income.		
(b)	The external auditor has a duty to ensure quality control procedures are in place within the audit practice and are implemented by their personnel.		

15 Tick the appropriate box for each of the following statements:

		True	False
(a)	External auditors are liable to anybody who relies solely on the audit report on financial statements when making investment decisions.		
(b)	External auditors may limit their liability to third parties if they include a disclaimer of liability in their audit report.		

16 Complete the following statement relating to the external auditor's liability.

An auditor can place a limit on the amount of damages payable by them in the event of a professional negligence claim. This is known as _____.

Select from: a liability cap, professional indemnity insurance.

ETHICAL ISSUES

17 **Identify, for each of the descriptions below, the concept it represents.**

(a) To comply with relevant laws and regulations and to avoid any action which discredits the profession. _____

(b) To ensure the auditor is far enough removed from the client to ensure that professional judgement can be in place. _____

Select from: Professional competence and due care, Professional behaviour, Independence, Objectivity

18 **Which one of the following situations is likely to give rise to a familiarity threat?**

Accepting a significant gift from an audit client.	
Owning shares in the client company.	
Acting as engagement partner of a listed audit client for more than 5 years.	

19 During the audit of Jesse Co, the audit senior discovered that the Managing Director Morris regularly pockets cash received from customers and does not include any details relating to the transaction in the accounting records of the business. Furthermore, none of this cash has been included as income on Morris' tax return.

Which one of the following is the appropriate action for the audit senior to take?

A The matter should be reported to the tax authorities after discussion with Morris.

B The matter should be reported to the tax authorities without discussion with Morris.

C The matter should be reported to your firm's money laundering reporting officer after discussion with Morris.

D The matter should be reported to your firm's money laundering reporting officer without discussion with Morris.

20 During the audit of Cayman Co, the audit senior discovered that during the year there was an issue of shares, all of which were bought by the Montego trust, based in the Bahamas. The senior made enquiries of the client as to the ownership and composition of this trust but was told that nobody except the Chairman knew anything about the trust. The chairman is currently taking a 2 month holiday in the Bahamas.

Which one of the following is the appropriate action for the audit senior to take?

A The matter should be reported to the CEO of Cayman Co immediately.

B The matter should be reported to the CEO of Cayman Co after discussions with the audit manager.

C The matter should be reported to the firm's money laundering officer after discussion with the CEO.

D The matter should be reported to the firm's money laundering office without discussion with the CEO.

21   Identify the threat posed by each of these situations.

	Self-interest	Self-review	Familiarity
Performance of internal and external audits of the same client.			
Overdue fees are outstanding from the client.			
The audit engagement partner and the Finance Director of the client are close friends.			

SAFEGUARDS

22   Below are statements regarding potential safeguards to be applied to protect an external auditor's independence and objectivity.

Identify whether each statement below is true or false.

Statement	True	False
When providing both internal and external audit services to a client, the assurance firm should use the same personnel for each of the assignments.		
The rotation of audit staff is an appropriate safeguard to mitigate a familiarity threat because the audit team has been in place for a number of years.		

23   Below are statements regarding potential safeguards to be applied to protect an external auditor's independence and objectivity.

Identify whether each statement below is true or false.

Statement	True	False
Declining an opportunity to prepare a listed company's financial statements as well as doing the audit is an appropriate safeguard to the self-review threat.		
The rotation of audit staff is an appropriate safeguard to mitigate an advocacy threat when the auditor is representing the audit client in court.		

CONFIDENTIALITY

24 There are certain circumstances in which an external auditor must or may disclose confidential information relating to a client. Some circumstances require the client's permission, whilst others do not.

Identify whether each of the following circumstances requires the external auditor to obtain the client's permission in order to disclose the information.

	Requires the client's permission	Does NOT require the client's permission
The external auditor suspects that the client is involved in money laundering.		
The provision of evidence to support the external auditor in court.		
The provision of information as requested by the client's bank.		

25 There are certain circumstances in which an external auditor must or may disclose confidential information relating to a client. Some circumstances require the client's permission, whilst others do not.

Identify whether each of the following circumstances requires the external auditor to obtain the client's permission in order to disclose the information.

	Requires the client's permission	Does NOT require the client's permission
A request to access the previous auditor's working papers in relation to a new client.		
The external auditor suspects that the client is involved in tax evasion.		
The external auditor suspects that a junior member of staff is involved in money laundering.		

26 The audit junior was overheard speaking to a friend in the pub after work one evening about the current audit he is on.

His friend works for a rival audit firm and they were discussing work that they had been involved in and the audit plan, approach to work and testing procedures.

Which two of the following would be appropriate action for the audit senior to take?

A   Report the audit junior to the client.

B   Advise the audit junior they must keep all information about the client private.

C   Invite the friend to join your audit firm.

D   Ensure full training is given to your audit junior on client confidentiality and security of sensitive information.

E   Make a formal complaint to the rival firm about the junior's friend.

27 While working on the audit of Weed Co, the audit junior decided to take home some of the working papers to help him better understand the financial statements.

However, shortly after starting to review them a friend called around and started to look at the statements with the junior to give his own opinion.

His friend works for a rival audit firm and mentioned this to his audit senior at work the next day.

Which two of the following would be appropriate action for the audit senior to take?

A   Report the audit junior to the client.

B   Advise the audit junior that he must not tell anyone about this.

C   Ask the audit junior to disclose the fees being charged by their competitors.

D   Ensure full training is given to your audit junior on client confidentiality and security of sensitive information.

INTERNAL CONTROL ENVIRONMENT

28 When evaluating internal controls of an audit client, the external auditor needs to understand a number of technical terms.

For each of the descriptions below, identify the technical term to which it relates.

The allocation of responsibilities within a process to different members of staff.	
The overall attitude of management about control and how important it is to the company.	
The part of the entity that performs activities designed to evaluate and improve internal controls and implement a risk management process.	

Select from: Control environment, External audit, Segregation of duties, Collusion, Internal audit, Risk assessment process

29   When evaluating internal controls of an audit client, the external auditor needs to understand a number of technical terms.

For each of the descriptions below, identify the technical term to which it relates.

The process of identifying the main issues facing a company.	
Responsible for assessing internal controls to determine if reliance is going to be placed on them.	
Members of staff acting together to defraud the company.	

Select from: Control environment, External audit, Segregation of duties, Collusion, Internal audit, Risk assessment process

CONTROL OBJECTIVES, RISKS AND PROCEDURES

30   Accounting systems have features such as control objectives and control procedures to mitigate the risk that a control objective is not met.

For each of the following select whether they are a control objective, risk or control procedure using the drop down menu.

	Control objective	Risk	Control procedure
(a) Receivables statements are only sent out if cash flow is poor.			
(b) Invoices for goods received are checked to orders and GRN before payment.			
(c) The debtor recoverability period is targeted at reducing the overall aged receivables to under 50 days.			

31   Accounting systems have features such as control objectives and control procedures to mitigate the risk that a control objective is not met.

For each of the following select whether they are a control objective, risk or control procedure using the drop down menu.

	Control objective	Risk	Control procedure
(a) Customers fail to pay for goods received.			
(b) All goods leaving the warehouse are invoiced.			
(c) Sequence check on delivery note numbers.			

32 Accounting systems have features such as control objectives and control procedures to mitigate the risk that a control objective is not met.

For each of the following select whether they are a control objective, risk or control procedure using the drop down menu.

	Control objective	Risk	Control procedure
(a) Damaged goods are accepted into the business.			
(b) All overtime is approved by managers before submission to the payroll.			
(c) The sales ledger control account reconciliation is signed by the Financial Controller each month.			

33 Accounting systems have features such as control objectives and control procedures to mitigate the risk that a control objective is not met.

For each of the following select whether they are a control objective, risk or control procedure using the drop down menu.

	Control objective	Risk	Control procedure
(a) Invoices are reconciled to supplier statements with no other checks on the validity of figures undertaken.			
(b) All orders are approved by the Department Head before being placed.			
(c) Invoices are only paid for goods received.			

ACCOUNTING SYSTEMS

34 The internal control checklist for Brown Co indicates that the Finance Director reviews the monthly payroll before it is paid.

Identify whether or not this would provide assurance on each of the following control objectives.

Control objective	Assurance provided	No assurance provided
Wages are only paid to genuine employees.		
The payroll is complete and contains the names of all employees.		

35 The internal control checklist for Green Co indicates that monthly cyclical inventory counts are undertaken. During the counts, a sample of inventory is counted and the condition of the sample inventory is reviewed.

Identify whether or not this would provide assurance on each of the following control objectives.

Control objective	Assurance provided	No assurance provided
Obsolete inventory is identified on a timely basis.		
Inventory is valued correctly at the lower of cost and net realisable value.		

36 The following are descriptions of procedures within the payroll system of Morley & Co.

For each procedure select whether it is a strength or weakness.

	Strength	Weakness
(a) The manual payroll is processed weekly by Alison who is also responsible for updating employee details such as the addition and deletion of employees and any changes to wage rates.		
(b) The Managing Director insists on reviewing a full payroll listing to authorise before he signs the cheque to withdraw the funds from the bank to pay the staff.		
(c) All timesheets, including overtime, are authorised and signed by line managers prior to be sent to the payroll department.		

37 The following are descriptions of procedures within the sales system of Nanny Plum & Co.

For each procedure select whether it is a strength or weakness.

	Strength	Weakness
(a) Customer credit limits are not subject to a regular review and if an urgent order is placed this is despatched without reference to current outstanding credit.		
(b) New customers can only obtain goods up to a set order limit and new orders are not despatched until the account is cleared for a period of two months until a credit history is established.		
(c) Sales orders are matched to Goods Despatch Notes and sales invoices. Sales orders are regularly reviewed to identify any unmatched orders.		

38 The following are descriptions of procedures within the accounting system of Wilson & Co.

For each procedure select whether it is a strength or weakness.

	Strength	Weakness
(a) The purchasing manager is responsible for all of the stages involved in the purchasing and verifying of goods.		
(b) Any changes to staff salaries are notified in writing from the relevant manager to the payroll manager.		
(c) Goods are despatched with no checks taking place on their condition, quantity or completeness.		

39 The following are descriptions of procedures within the payroll system of Tages & Co.

For each procedure select whether it is a strength or weakness.

	Strength	Weakness
(a) The computerised payroll is processed weekly by Larissa who is also responsible for amending the standing data details such as the addition of new employees and changes to wage rates.		
(b) The Managing Director, Adam, reviews the BACs listing of net pay details per employee and signs the listing before authorising the assistant accountant, Marie, to transmit the details to the company's bank.		

40 The following are descriptions of procedures within the sales system of Lemon Limes & Co.

For each procedure select whether it is a strength or weakness.

	Strength	Weakness
(a) Any discounts from standard selling prices that the sales team would like to offer clients must be approved first by Leo Lemon, the Sales Director.		
(b) Credit notes are not part of the sales system and are raised manually on a word processor by any of the sales administrators.		

RISKS AND CONTROLS

41 An entity uses internal control procedures in order to mitigate the risks to which the entity is exposed. Listed below are two internal control procedures which are applicable to an entity's inventory procurement system.

For each internal control procedure use drag and drop to match the procedure with the risk mitigated.

(a) Invoice matched to goods received note.

(b) An agreed reorder level is established for inventory that is regularly reviewed by the warehouse manager.

Select from: Purchasing goods from unauthorised suppliers, Theft of inventory, Purchasing unnecessary goods, Paying for goods not received

42 An entity uses internal control procedures in order to mitigate the risks to which the entity is exposed. Listed below are two internal control procedures which are applicable to an entity's sales system.

For each internal control procedure use drag and drop to match the procedure with the risk mitigated.

(a) Credit checks are carried out on new customers before orders are accepted.

(b) Credit levels are set for customers which are regularly reviewed to ensure they are not exceeded.

Select from: Customers receiving goods that they cannot pay for, Risk of running out of inventory, Customers exceeding credit terms set, Aged receivables affecting cash flow

43 An entity uses internal control procedures in order to mitigate the risks to which the entity is exposed. Listed below are two internal control procedures which are applicable to an entity's payroll system.

For each internal control procedure use drag and drop to match the procedure with the risk mitigated.

(a) Timesheets completed by production staff are checked and signed by the production director before being submitted to payroll.

(b) A monthly review of payroll reports is carried out by a director to verify pay details and contracted hours.

Select from: Employee personal details verified, Sickness levels not recorded, Staff paid for hours not worked, inaccurate wage rates and deductions.

44 An entity uses internal control procedures in order to mitigate the risks to which the entity is exposed. Listed below are two internal control procedures which are applicable to an entity's inventory procurement system.

For each internal control procedure use drag and drop to match the procedure with the risk mitigated.

(a) Purchase invoices matched to goods received records prior to posting to the ledger.

(b) Physical counts of inventory and reconciliation with recorded amounts.

Select from: Purchasing goods from unauthorised suppliers, Theft of inventory, Purchasing unnecessary goods, Paying for goods not received.

45 An entity uses internal control procedures in order to mitigate the risks to which the entity is exposed. Listed below are two internal control procedures which are applicable to an entity's payroll system.

For each internal control procedure use drag and drop to match the procedure with the risk mitigated.

(a) Only the Finance Director has the password to amend standing data.

(b) Departmental Managers submit a list of all approved overtime to payroll in addition to it being included on timesheets.

Select from: Paying the same employee twice in the same period, paying for overtime that was never worked, Changing people's salaries or diverting money in to a different bank account, forgetting to pay a new employee in their first month.

VERIFICATION TECHNIQUES

46 **Identify whether the following procedures are tests of control, tests of detail or analytical procedures.**

Procedure	Test of control	Test of detail	Analytical procedure
Developing an expectation of payroll costs by taking into account last year's payroll figure, annual pay rises and starters and leavers.			
Reviewing purchase orders to see if they have been approved by a relevant member of staff.			
Recalculating PAYE and NIC costs for payroll.			
Calculating receivables and payables days and comparing to the prior year.			
Reviewing bank reconciliations to ensure they have been prepared and reviewed by an appropriate person.			

47 As part of verification techniques in respect of sales and receivables, an auditor will inspect sales invoices. The auditor will gain assurance about different assertions depending on the information on the invoice.

In respect of the information below, select the assertion for which that information will provide assurance using the drop down menu.

	Accuracy	Classification	Existence
(a) Receivables circularisation letter			
(b) After date receipts			
(c) Description of goods			

48 As part of verification techniques in respect of purchases, an auditor will carry out the following tests to confirm existence, valuation or completeness.

In respect of the information below, select the assertion for which that information will provide assurance using the drop down menu.

	Valuation	Completeness	Existence
(a) The auditor seeks assurance that the asset or liability is recorded at the correct value.			
(b) A full inventory check is performed with the auditor verifying inventory sheets to inventory on shelves.			

49 As part of verification techniques in respect of purchases, an auditor will inspect purchase invoices. The auditor will gain assurance about different assertions depending on the information on the invoice.

In respect of the information below, select the assertion for which that information will provide assurance using the drop down menu.

	Accuracy	Classification	Cut-off	Existence
(a) Date of the invoice.				
(b) Description of the item purchased.				
(c) Monetary amount.				

50   As part of verification techniques in respect of purchases, an auditor will inspect purchase invoices. The auditor will gain assurance about different assertions depending on the information within those documents.

In respect of the information below, select the assertion for which that information will provide assurance using the drop down menu.

	Rights and obligations	Cut-off	Valuation	Classification
(a) Addressee of the invoice.				
(b) Date of the goods received note.				
(c) Description of the item.				

COMPUTER-ASSISTED AUDIT TECHNIQUES

51   Two types of computer-assisted audit techniques (CAAT) are test data and audit software.

For each of the procedures listed below, select the type of CAAT which would be used to perform that procedure using the drop down menu.

	Test data	Audit software
(a) The stratification of data to perform full audit testing.		
(b) Input of data with false dates to check the system identifies incorrect data for the period.		
(c) The identification of a missing sequence in source documents.		

52   Two types of computer-assisted audit techniques (CAAT) are test data and audit software.

For each of the procedures listed below, select the type of CAAT which would be used to perform that procedure using the drop down menu.

	Test data	Audit software
(a) To test that timesheets are not input for non-existent employees.		
(b) To carry out statistical analysis of data within the population.		
(c) To check the accuracy of calculations within a spreadsheet.		

53 Two types of computer-assisted audit techniques (CAAT) are test data and audit software.

For each of the procedures listed below, select the type of CAAT which would be used to perform that procedure using the drop down menu.

	Test data	Audit software
(a) The auditor enters fictitious data into the computer system and carries out checks that the application controls the system should run have operated as expected.		
(b) The technique is used to examine the client's accounting data including identifying trends and producing aged analysis.		
(c) The auditor will look to highlight suspicious items according to pre-determined search criteria.		

54 Two types of computer-assisted audit techniques (CAAT) are test data and audit software.

For each of the procedures listed below, select the type of CAAT which would be used to perform that procedure using the drop down menu.

	Test data	Audit software
(a) Comparison of the cost and net realisable value of inventory items to determine the lower value.		
(b) Input of data with false inventory code numbers to check that the system rejects such data.		
(c) Extraction of inventory balances over £5,000 in order to carry out further testing.		

55 Two types of computer-assisted audit techniques (CAAT) are test data and audit software.

For each of the procedures listed below, select the type of CAAT which would be used to perform that procedure using the drop down menu.

	Test data	Audit software
(a) Calculating a statistically significant sample size for testing the receivables population.		
(b) Inputting a credit card into an e-commerce sales system which has gone beyond its expiry date.		
(c) Attempting to assign a VAT rate of greater than 20% to a sales transaction.		

SAMPLING

56   **Identify the technical term for each of the descriptions below.**

(a)   A sampling approach whereby items are chosen in a sequential order._____

(b)   A sampling approach whereby items are selected with a constant interval between selections._____

(c)   The risk that the auditor misinterprets the audit evidence obtained._____

Select from: Stratification, Block sampling, Systematic sampling, Haphazard sampling, Sampling risk, Non-sampling risk

57   When selecting items in order to perform tests of detail, the external auditor has to consider a number of factors.

Identify whether the following factors will result in an increase in sample size, a decrease in sample size or have a negligible effect on sample size.

	Increase	Decrease	No effect
Being able to test very easily 90% of the sales invoices by way of a proof in total.			
Internal controls are found to be weak and not operating effectively.			
The audit client requesting that the auditor reduces the amount of testing.			

TESTS OF CONTROL AND SUBSTANTIVE PROCEDURES

58   The external auditor may adopt an audit approach which involves undertaking either:

- tests of controls and substantive procedures, or

- substantive procedures only, with no tests of controls.

Identify the most likely approach to be adopted by the external auditor in each of the following circumstances.

	Tests of controls and substantive procedures	Substantive procedures only, with no tests of controls
The audited entity was only set up a year ago, and there is only one member of staff in the accounting department.		
There is no segregation of duties within the accounting department of the client.		
The client has an internal audit department which reviews controls throughout the year.		

59   The external auditor may adopt an audit approach which involves undertaking either:

- •   tests of controls and substantive procedures, or

- •   substantive procedures only, with no tests of controls.

Identify the most likely approach to be adopted by the external auditor in each of the following circumstances.

	Tests of controls and substantive procedures	Substantive procedures only, with no tests of controls
The entity has a strong control environment.		
A large fraud has been identified which came about due to the collusion of several members of staff.		
A new accounting package was introduced at the beginning of the year and there have been significant operational deficiencies with the new system.		

60   Auditors use tests of controls and substantive procedures to gather audit evidence.

For each of the procedures listed below, select whether it is a test of control or a substantive procedure using the drop down menu.

	Test of control	Substantive procedure
(a) The distribution and reviewing of receivables circularisation letters.		
(b) Reviewing credit control procedures for recoverability of receivables.		
(c) Reconcile a sample of debit entries recorded in the ledger and agree to the purchase day book.		

61   Auditors use tests of controls and substantive procedures to gather audit evidence.

For each of the procedures listed below, select whether it is a test of control or a substantive procedure using the drop down menu.

	Test of control	Substantive procedure
(a) Perform tests on the supplier statement reconciliation process to confirm the completeness of payables.		
(b) To carry out checks on the accuracy of recording invoices for prices, discounts, VAT calculation and totals.		
(c) To verify that a transaction or event took place which pertains to the entity during the relevant period.		

62   Auditors use tests of controls and substantive procedures to gather audit evidence.

For each of the procedures listed below, select whether it is a test of control or a substantive procedure using the drop down menu.

	Test of control	Substantive procedure
(a) Comparison of the current year's revenue figure with the previous year's figure.		
(b) Observation of the despatch procedures in respect of goods leaving an entity's warehouse.		
(c) Vouching of an addition to non-current assets to the supplier's invoice.		

ACCOUNT BALANCES AND ASSOCIATED RISKS

63   The external auditor is required to undertake analytical procedures as part of the planning process in order to identify the risk of misstatement of figures in the financial statements. The results of the analytical procedures conducted on trade receivables and trade payables in the financial statements of an audit client are listed below.

Select whether the results indicate that trade receivables and trade payables might have been under or overstated using the drop down menu.

	Understated	Overstated
(a) The results show that compared to the previous year trade receivables has increased by 30% and revenue has increased by 9%.		
(b) The results show that compared to the previous year trade payables has decreased by 15% and purchases have decreased by 10%.		

64   The external auditor is required to undertake analytical procedures as part of the planning process in order to identify the risk of misstatement of figures in the financial statements. The results of the analytical procedures conducted on trade receivables and trade payables in the financial statements of an audit client are listed below.

Select whether the results indicate that trade receivables and trade payables might have been under or overstated using the drop down menu.

	Understated	Overstated
(a) The results show that compared to the previous year trade receivables has increased by 20% and revenue has increased by 5%.		
(b) The results show that compared to the previous year trade payables has decreased by 10% and purchases have decreased by 7%.		

AUDIT RISK

65 Audit risk is the risk that the auditor expresses an inappropriate opinion either on the financial statements as a whole or in relation to a particular financial area.

Select which of the following are components of the audit risk model that must be utilised by the auditor.

	Yes	No
Inherent risk		
Control risk		
Identity risk		
Detection risk		

66 **Complete the following statement on audit risk and its component parts, by filling in the gaps using drag and drop.**

The auditor, during his planning, must assess the level of audit risk and its component parts.

(a) _____ is the risk that a client's internal controls have not detected a material misstatement.

(b) _____ is the risk that the auditor's procedures do not detect a material misstatement in the financial statements.

(c) _____ is the risk of the auditor issuing an incorrect audit opinion.

(d) _____ is the risk of there being a material misstatement in the financial statements due to the nature of the client.

Select from: Audit risk, Inherent risk, Control risk, Detection risk

67 Control risk is a key component of the audit risk model.

Select whether the following actions would be likely to increase or decrease the control risk in relation to sales using the drop down menu.

	Increase	Decrease
(a) Sales invoices are only raised for goods that have been dispatched.		
(b) No initial credit checks are made on new customers to gauge their creditworthiness.		
(c) All customer receipts are correctly recorded.		

68 Internal controls are designed to ensure the efficient conduct of an entity, the safeguarding of assets, detection of fraud and error and the accuracy and completeness of the accounting records.

Select whether the following will be likely to increase or decrease the reliability of a client's internal controls in affecting the risk of misstatement or fraud using the drop down menu.

	Increase	Decrease
(a) Due to cost saving measures, there is less segregation of duties amongst the payroll staff.		
(b) The entity has recently introduced a new cash handling procedure with complete procedure notes distributed to all staff.		
(c) Management regularly review budgets and compare to forecasts to analyse the company's performance.		

69 **Tick the appropriate box for each of the following statements:**

	True	False
(a) External auditors are able to control inherent risk and control risk so as to reduce audit risk to an acceptably low level.		
(b) External auditors are able to control detection risk so as to reduce audit risk to an acceptably low level.		

70 When planning an audit of financial statements, the external auditor is required to consider how factors such as the entity's operating environment and its system of internal control affect the risk of misstatement in the financial statements.

Select whether the following factors are likely to increase, decrease, or have no effect on the risk of misstatement using the drop down menu.

	Increase	Decrease	No effect
(a) The entity is committed to employing personnel with appropriate accounting and financial reporting skills.			
(b) The entity is to be sold and the purchase consideration will be determined as a multiple of reported profit.			
(c) The entity's management does not intend to remedy deficiencies in internal controls identified by the external auditor.			

MATERIALITY

71 **Tick the appropriate box for each of the following statements:**

	True	False
(a) As part of the audit planning, the auditor will determine the maximum amount of errors he is willing to accept and still be satisfied that the financial statements show a true and fair view.		
(b) Materiality is equally important to the auditor when expressing an opinion and the management when reviewing the financial statements.		

72 **Tick the appropriate box for each of the following statements:**

	True	False
(a) A material error in the financial statements may be described as the relative significance or importance of a particular matter in the context of the financial statements.		
(b) A material error in the financial statements may be described as a lack of robust written processes and procedures in place to record each stage of a transaction.		

73 **Tick the appropriate box for each of the following statements:**

	True	False
(a) Materiality is not capable of general mathematical definition as it has both qualitative and quantitative aspects.		
(b) The auditor will consider a relatively small error in a month end procedure an indication of a potential material misstatement if that error is repeated each month.		

74 **Tick the appropriate box for each of the following statements:**

	True	False
(a) When determining materiality, the auditor just looks at the size of an item in comparison to the profit of the client.		
(b) Auditing standards specify what percentage of profit would make an item material.		

75 **Tick the appropriate box for each of the following statements:**

	True	False
(a) Performance materiality is set a level above materiality as it only relates to the financial statements as a whole.		
(b) The idea behind performance materiality is to reduce to an acceptably low level the probability that the aggregate uncorrected and undetected misstatements exceed materiality for the financial statements as a whole.		

76 Tick the appropriate box for each of the following statements:

	True	False
(a) Performance materiality should be set at a level below the level of materiality for the financial statements as a whole.		
(b) Once established, performance materiality must not be changed as the audit progresses.		

77 Tick the appropriate box for each of the following statements:

	True	False
(a) Performance materiality is always a given percentage of overall materiality.		
(b) All errors found, in excess of performance materiality, must be amended by the client in order to avoid the audit report being qualified.		

INFORMATION AND RECOMMENDATIONS FOR THE AUDIT PLAN

78 You are planning the audit of Top Notch Co (Top Notch), a chain of hairdressing salons in the Midlands.

Top Notch employs 40 staff throughout the region. The majority of staff are paid weekly via BACs transfer. However, a small number of casual weekend staff are paid cash in hand on a weekly basis.

Approximately half of Top Notch's customers pay by credit or debit card, with the remainder paying in cash. Cash is banked weekly by the Salon Manager and a note is sent to Head Office with the amount banked. No other checks of the tills are carried out.

Each salon purchases its own goods (shampoo, conditioner etc.) from local suppliers. Invoices are sent directly to Head Office, without any check by the individual salon. Any larger capital purchases must be authorised by Head Office.

Identify and explain the audit risks relating to the external audit of Top Notch Co. Where possible, your answer should refer to specific items in the financial statements which may be at risk of misstatement.

79 You are planning the audit of Florida Air Conditioning (FAC).

FAC is a privately owned business, run by two brothers. The company was set up in 2001 and has been very successful and now employs 60 staff.

FAC has two income streams:

- sale of air conditioning units, and

- provision of air conditioning service support contracts (vary from 1 – 3 years).

Customers are invoiced after installation of air conditioning units. Customers are invoiced annually in advance for service support contracts.

FAC manufactures its air conditioning units in house. FAC's inventory consists of finished units, part finished units (work in progress) and component parts used for the production of units and spares for the service contracts. FAC sources some of the component parts for its units from an overseas supplier and must pay these invoices in the supplier's local currency.

FAC offer a 1 year warranty on all new purchases of air conditioning units. The company has included a warranty provision on the Statement of Financial Position and it is material to the financial statements.

Identify and explain the audit risks relating to the external audit of Florida Air Conditioning. Where possible, your answer should refer to specific items in the financial statements which may be at risk of misstatement.

80   During the year ended 31 December 20X2, Green Co took out a bank loan of £1 million to fund a capital project. The terms of the loan require:

- Capital repayments, over 5 years, in monthly instalments commencing 1 July 20X2

- Interest at 9% per annum payable monthly.

- Profit before interest and tax in the monthly management accounts to cover interest at least four times.

Set out, in a manner suitable for inclusion in the audit plan the audit risks relating to the loan.

81   During the year ended 31 December 20X2, Pepco Co acquired a fleet of 10 new lorries for distribution, at a cost of £7m, payable in 3 annual instalments on a finance agreement at 8%.

Set out, in a manner suitable for inclusion in the audit plan the audit risks relating to the finance agreement and related non-current assets.

82   Tileclose Co is a civil engineering company that provides a pipe-laying service to the energy, water and telecommunications industries. It uses much heavy plant and machinery, and is subject to the strict provisions of Health and Safety at work regulations.

Set out, in a manner suitable for inclusion in the audit plan the audit risks relating to Tileclose Co.

VERIFICATION OF ITEMS IN THE FINANCIAL STATEMENTS

83   Smart Sense Co is a small company which undertakes the installation and upgrade of computer software under short-term fixed-price contracts.

All direct costs incurred that relate to each contract are recorded in the company's job costing system which is fully integrated with the purchases and payroll applications.

The Financial Controller uses the job costing records to estimate the value of work in progress for the monthly management accounts and the year-end financial statements.

Set out, in a manner suitable for inclusion in the audit plan, the audit procedures to be undertaken in order to ensure that work in progress is fairly stated in the financial statements.

84 During the audit of Short Circuit Co, a computer manufacturing company, the audit junior asks how it is possible to establish the existence, completeness and ownership of the company's non-current assets.

Set out, in a manner suitable for inclusion in the audit plan, the audit procedures to be undertaken in order to gather evidence to support these issues and ensure the assets are fairly stated in the financial statements.

85 Honeysuckle Co is a company which hires out various items of equipment to a range of customers ranging from small contractors to very large building companies. The hire periods range from one day to six months and there is a great variety in the number of items hired at any one time per customer. For individual items and hire periods of less than one month, Honeysuckle Co issues an invoice on completion of the hire period. For hire periods greater than one month a progress invoice is issued at each month end. The credit period is 30 days.

Set out, in a manner suitable for inclusion in the audit plan, the audit procedures to be undertaken in order to ensure that receivables are fairly stated in the financial statements.

AUDIT DOCUMENTATION

86 Audit documentation serves a number of purposes.

Identify the purpose of each of the working papers in the table below by dragging the appropriate reason for preparation next to each working paper. Each answer option can be used more than once or not at all.

Working paper	Reason for preparation
Independence questionnaire completed by each member of the audit team.	
Copies of cash flow and profit forecasts and post year-end management accounts.	
Details of the review of assets in the factory whilst attending the inventory count.	

Select from: Assess the going concern status, Compliance with independence and ethical requirements, Supporting valuation of assets

87 **Tick the appropriate box for each of the following statements:**

	True	False
(a) Working papers must only be prepared in electronic form to ensure confidentiality and security.		
(b) There are two main types of file for audit working papers; the permanent audit file and the current audit file.		
(c) The date of the working papers and the name of the person preparing the file should be clearly stated on all documents.		

88 **Tick the appropriate box for each of the following statements:**

	True	False
(a) The audit working papers are prepared and collated during the audit and should be retained in connection with the performance of the audit.		
(b) The permanent audit file should not contain any copies of statutory or legal regulations or papers.		
(c) The current audit file should include schedules showing the results of audit tests carried out.		

89 **Tick the appropriate box for each of the following statements:**

	True	False
(a) The auditor's working papers provide adequate evidence of the work that has been carried out and the conclusions reached contain sufficient appropriate audit evidence to support the conclusions made.		
(b) The auditor will rely on a designated staff member from the client's workforce to assist in the compilation of the current audit file.		
(c) The permanent audit files contain information of continuing importance to the audit such as board minutes of relevance, previous years' signed accounts analytical reviews and engagement letters.		

90 **Tick the appropriate box for each of the following statements:**

	True	False
(a) Working papers are prepared by the external auditor because there is a legal requirement to do so.		
(b) The objective of working papers is to provide evidence that the audit was planned and performed in accordance with International Standards on Auditing.		
(c) Working papers should contain the name of who performed the audit work and the date it was performed.		

91 **Tick the appropriate box for each of the following statements:**

	True	False
(a) The detailed content of each type of audit working paper is strictly detailed in the ISAs.		
(b) The primary objective of working papers is to prove to the audit partner that the work was done.		
(c) Working papers should clearly state which year-end they pertain to and show evidence that they have been reviewed.		

IDENTIFY MATTERS OF AN UNUSUAL NATURE

92   When carrying out the audit of Beach Co, the audit junior has carried out the bank reconciliation process for a sample month and has noticed a number of transactions for cash withdrawals that have no supporting documentation.

The manager informed the audit junior that this type of transaction was necessary for the day to day running of the business and not everyone could remember to obtain receipts or supporting documentation.

The value of the withdrawals has increased significantly throughout the period and the audit junior believes it may be significant in the financial statements.

In respect of this matter, select the appropriate response using the drop down menu.

No further action	Refer to supervisor

93   When carrying out the audit of Sunshine Co, the audit junior has documented an invoice for the cost of family holiday for the Managing Director.

The purchase ledger clerk informed the audit junior that this type of invoice is received on a regular basis with the instruction to include the costs in general expenses.

The value of the invoice for the holiday is immaterial in terms of key figures in the financial statements.

In respect of this matter, select the appropriate response using the drop down menu.

No further action	Refer to supervisor

94   During the external audit of Prep Co, the audit junior identified an invoice for the cost of school fees for the Managing Director's children. The purchase ledger clerk informed the audit junior that the Managing Director had told her to hide the costs in sundries. The amount of the school fees is insignificant in terms of key figures in the financial statements.

In respect of this matter, select the appropriate response using the drop down menu.

No further action	Refer to supervisor

95   During the external audit of Dodge Co, the audit junior identified a number of occurrences where mileage claims were processed through the payroll for staff that did not appear on the approved mileage list supplied by the payroll manager.

The ledger clerk said that there were valid reasons for these expenses but could not give any specifics.

The values were not of a material nature and discussions with the payroll manager indicated that systems had been put in place to eliminate this in the future.

In respect of this matter, select the appropriate response using the drop down menu.

No further action	Refer to supervisor

96   During the external audit of Sike Co, the audit junior identified two instances where a number of time sheets were not signed by the Payroll Manager prior to being processed through the monthly pay process and posting to the ledger. Both instances occurred when the payroll supervisor who is responsible for verifying the documents was on annual leave. Subsequent further tests indicated no similar weakness following his return to work.

In respect of this matter, select the appropriate response using the drop down menu.

No further action	Refer to supervisor

97   During the external audit of Trike Co, the audit junior identified a number of occurrences where the financial data entered into the computer spreadsheets was incorrectly input, with some of the errors causing material differences in the financial statements.

The junior has also noted that there is no virus protection on the computers used to generate the financial statements and that staff regularly use this computer to download games, and log onto social networking sites.

In respect of this matter, select the appropriate response using the drop down menu.

No further action	Refer to supervisor

98   During the external audit of Jemima Co, the audit junior identified two instances of failure to authorise purchase invoices prior to posting to the purchase ledger. Both instances occurred when the purchase supervisor who is responsible for authorising such transactions was away on sick leave, and further tests indicated no similar failings following her return to work.

In respect of this matter, select the appropriate response using the drop down menu.

No further action	Refer to supervisor

99   During the external audit of Perch Co, the audit junior was requested to add up 10 pages of the cash book from throughout the year. 9 of the pages added up correctly but one page had a transposition error leading to it being under cast by £69.

The turnover of Perch Co was £3.5m for the year and the profit was £469,000.

In respect of this matter, select the appropriate response using the drop down menu.

No further action	Refer to supervisor

DRAFT REPORTS AND RECOMMENDATIONS

100   During the audit of Pump Co, it was discovered that although the company maintained a non-current asset register to record the details of its sports and fitness equipment, no checking procedures other than reconciliation with the nominal ledger are undertaken.

Prepare extracts, suitable for inclusion in a report to management of Pump Co, which set out

(a)   **the possible consequences; and**

(b)   **the recommendations that you would make in respect of this matter.**

101   Delta Co's sales invoices are produced by its computer system using the relevant price held as standing data on the sales master file. Selling prices are updated by the sales ledger clerk on the verbal authority of the Sales Director.

Prepare extracts, suitable for inclusion in a report to management of Delta Co, which set out

(a)   **the possible consequences; and**

(b)   **the recommendations that you would make in respect of the matters outlined above.**

102   During the audit of Pharo Co, a manufacturing company, it was discovered that when goods other than raw materials arrive to the warehouse door, a member of the warehouse staff sends an email to the person they think the goods were intended for to ask them to come to the warehouse to pick them up. No other action is taken.

Prepare extracts, suitable for inclusion in a report to management of Pharo Co, which set out

(a)   **the possible consequences; and**

(b)   **the recommendations that you would make in respect of this matter.**

AUDIT REPORTS

103 The following statements detail opinions given by the auditor on the financial statements of two companies.

State whether the audit opinions detail a qualified opinion, unmodified opinion or disclaimer of opinion dependent on the statement.

	Qualified opinion	Unmodified opinion	Disclaimer of opinion
(a) In our opinion: The financial statements give a true and fair view, in accordance with UK Generally Accepted Accounting Practice, of the state of the company's affairs as at 31 March 2008 and of its profit for the year then ended. The financial statements have been properly prepared in accordance with the Companies Act 2006; and the information given in the Directors' Report is consistent with the financial statements.			
(b) Extract: I planned my audit so as to obtain all the information and explanations which I considered necessary in order to provide me with sufficient evidence to give reasonable assurance that the financial statements are free from material misstatements. In forming my opinion I also evaluated the overall adequacy of the presentation of information in the financial statements. However, the evidence available to me was limited by the fundamental uncertainties that meant I was unable to form an opinion on the financial statements. In the circumstances we are unable to form an audit opinion.			

104 During the audit of Wand Co, the audit senior discovered that the depreciation methods used by the management have changed twice during the accounting period.

The management refuse to give any details of the reasoning behind the changes and the auditor has not been able to obtain sufficient evidence to support the changes. In addition, the auditor believes that the treatment could lead to a material but not pervasive misstatement.

Which one of the following opinions is appropriate in the circumstances?

A   modified opinion due to an inability to obtain sufficient appropriate evidence

B   unmodified opinion; or

D   modified opinion due to a material misstatement.

105 **For the following situations select whether or not the audit opinion on the financial statements would be modified using the drop down menu.**

	Modified	Not modified
(a) Ash Co capitalised costs of £150,000 in respect of repairs and maintenance and included these costs in non-current assets. The amount capitalised represents 30% of Ash Co's profit before tax. The directors refuse to make any adjustments in respect of this matter.		
(b) There is a significant uncertainty about Medlar Co's ability to continue as a going concern. The directors of Medlar Co have prepared the financial statements on a going concern basis and have fully disclosed the uncertainty in the notes to the financial statements.		

106 **For each of the following situations which have arisen in two unrelated audit clients, select whether or not the audit opinion on the financial statements would be modified.**

	Modified	Not modified
(a) There is a claim against Santa Co which is waiting to go to court. The opinion of the Directors is that they are unlikely to have to pay any damages. The auditor agrees with this judgement. The Directors have made a full disclosure of this situation in the accounts. Although potentially material, the damages would not have a significant impact on the company.		
(b) Elves Co has a receivable which owes the company £125,000. No payments have been made on this debt for 6 months. This represents 20% of the overall receivables figure, 2% of revenue and 15% of profit for the year. The client refuses to provide for this amount as they believe that once the new management team at the client are settled in, regular payments will start to be made.		

107 For each of the following situations which have arisen in Alba Co, select the impact on the auditor's report on the financial statements.

	Adverse opinion	Unmodified opinion with a Material Uncertainty Related to Going Concern section included in the audit report	Unmodified opinion with an Emphasis of Matter paragraph
(a) The directors of Alba Co have produced a cash flow forecast which shows a significantly worsening position over the coming 12 months. The auditors have been informed that Alba's bankers will not make a decision on the renewal of the overdraft facility until after the auditor's report is completed. The directors have agreed to include some going concern disclosures. The auditor believes the disclosures made by the directors are adequate.			
(b) In relation to the above scenario, the auditor believes the basis of preparation of the financial statements is incorrect.			

Section 2

ANSWERS TO PRACTICE QUESTIONS

LEVEL OF ASSURANCE

1   The overall objectives of the external auditor are to obtain **reasonable** assurance about whether the financial statements are free from **material** misstatement, whether due to fraud or error, thereby enabling the auditor to **express an opinion** on whether the financial statements are prepared in all material respects in accordance with **an applicable financial framework.**

2

		True	False
(a)	Auditors aim to give absolute assurance over the accuracy of the financial statements.		✓
(b)	An audit includes examining, on a test basis, evidence supporting the amounts and disclosures in the financial statements.	✓	

3

Reasonable assurance	Limited assurance
✓	

LEGAL AND REGULATORY ISSUES

4

		True	False
(a)	The auditor must maintain professional scepticism throughout the duration of the audit.	✓	
(b)	The client must maintain their professional scepticism throughout the duration of the audit.		✓

5

	True	False
(a) Professional scepticism refers to the auditor not believing anything the client says to them.		✓
(b) Professional scepticism refers to the questioning mind the auditor should maintain.	✓	

6 It is the responsibility of the **directors** to prepare the annual financial statements for the company and it is the responsibility of the **external auditors** to report to **shareholders** whether in their opinion the financial statements show a **true and fair view**.

7 The most important professional attribute of an auditor is their **independence**. This enables the auditor **to express an opinion** as to the truth and fairness of the financial statements to the shareholders and gives assurance as to the **objectivity** of the auditor.

8

	True	False
(a) The auditors are responsible for preparing the financial statements on which they report.		✓
(b) The amounts in the financial statements are stated precisely.		✓
(c) The external auditor provides reasonable assurance on the future viability of the audited entity.		✓

9

	True	False
(a) The IAASB works to improve the uniformity of auditing practices exclusively in the UK.		✓
(b) The IAASB's standards contain basic principles and essential procedures together with related guidance in the form of explanatory and other material, including appendices.	✓	

10 **D**

The IAASB is responsible for setting auditing standards which facilitate the convergence of national and international auditing standards.

11 **C**

ISAs are mandatory on all audits undertaken in the countries which have adopted ISAs unless the auditor has good reason for non-compliance.

EXTERNAL AUDITOR'S LIABILITY

12

	True	False
(a) The primary duty of an auditor as set out in s235 of the Companies Act 2006 requires him to report to the company's members on every set of accounts requiring statutory audit.	✓	
(b) The external auditor has a statutory duty to detect fraud as part of the main duties of the audit.		✓

13

	True	False
(a) The external auditor has a common law duty of care towards certain third parties under the law of tort.	✓	
(b) The external auditor has a duty to exercise 'reasonable skill and care' to the client and any breach may lead to a claim of negligence by the client.	✓	

14

	True	False
(a) Professional Indemnity Insurance is compulsory for all members of the Institute who have a practising certificate and are engaged in public practice, regardless of the amount of practice income.	✓	
(b) The external auditor has a duty to ensure quality control procedures are in place within the audit practice and are implemented by their personnel.	✓	

15

	True	False
(a) External auditors are liable to anybody who relies solely on the audit report on financial statements when making investment decisions.		✓
(b) External auditors may limit their liability to third parties if they include a disclaimer of liability in their audit report.	✓	

16 An auditor can place a limit on the amount of damages payable by them in the event of a professional negligence claim. This is known as **a liability cap**.

ETHICAL ISSUES

17 (a) To comply with relevant laws and regulations and to avoid any action which discredits the profession. **Professional behaviour**

(b) To ensure the auditor is far enough removed from the client to ensure that professional judgement can be in place. **Independence**

18

Accepting a significant gift from an audit client.	
Owning shares in the client company.	
Acting as engagement partner of a listed audit client for more than 5 years.	✓

19 **D**

The matter should be reported to your firm's money laundering reporting officer without discussion with Morris.

20 **D**

The matter should be reported to the firm's money laundering office without discussion with the CEO.

21

	Self-interest	Self-review	Familiarity
Performance of internal and external audits of the same client.		✓	
Overdue fees are outstanding from the client.	✓		
The audit engagement partner and the Finance Director of the client are close friends.			✓

SAFEGUARDS

22

Statement	True	False
When providing both internal and external audit services to a client, the assurance firm should use the same personnel for each of the assignments.		✓
The rotation of audit staff is an appropriate safeguard to mitigate a familiarity threat because the audit team has been in place for a number of years.	✓	

23

Statement	True	False
Declining an opportunity to prepare a listed company's financial statements as well as doing the audit is an appropriate safeguard to the self-review threat.	✓	
The rotation of audit staff is an appropriate safeguard to mitigate an advocacy threat when the auditor is representing the audit client in court.		✓

CONFIDENTIALITY

24

	Requires the client's permission	Does NOT require the client's permission
The external auditor suspects that the client is involved in money laundering.		✓
The provision of evidence to support the external auditor in court.		✓
The provision of information as requested by the client's bank.	✓	

25

	Requires the client's permission	Does NOT require the client's permission
A request to access the previous auditor's working papers in relation to a new client.	✓	
The external auditor suspects that the client is involved in tax evasion.		✓
The external auditor suspects that a junior member of staff is involved in money laundering.		✓

26   B and D

Advise the audit junior they must keep all information about the client private.

Ensure full training is given to your audit junior on client confidentiality and security of sensitive information.

27   A and D

Report the audit junior to the client to make them aware of what has happened.

Ensure full training is given to your audit junior on client confidentiality and security of sensitive information.

INTERNAL CONTROL ENVIRONMENT

28

The allocation of responsibilities within a process to different members of staff.	Segregation of duties
The overall attitude of management about control and how important it is to the company.	Control environment
The part of the entity that performs activities designed to evaluate and improve internal controls and implement a risk management process.	Internal audit

29

The process of identifying the main issues facing a company.	Risk assessment process
Responsible for assessing internal controls to determine if reliance is going to be placed on them.	External audit
Members of staff acting together to defraud the company.	Collusion

CONTROL OBJECTIVES, RISKS AND PROCEDURES

30

	Control objective	Risk	Control procedure
(a) Receivables statements are only sent out if cash flow is poor.		✓	
(b) Invoices for goods received are checked to orders and GRN before payment.			✓
(c) The debtor recoverability period is targeted at reducing the overall aged receivables to under 50 days.	✓		

31

	Control objective	Risk	Control procedure
(a) Customers fail to pay for goods received.		✓	
(b) All goods leaving the warehouse are invoiced.	✓		
(c) Sequence check on delivery note numbers.			✓

32

	Control objective	Risk	Control procedure
(a) Damaged goods are accepted into the business.		✓	
(b) All overtime is approved by managers before submission to the payroll.			✓
(c) The sales ledger control account reconciliation is signed by the Financial Controller each month.			✓

33

	Control objective	Risk	Control procedure
(a) Invoices are reconciled to supplier statements with no other checks on the validity of figures undertaken.		✓	
(b) All orders are approved by the Department Head before being placed.			✓
(c) Invoices are only paid for goods received.	✓		

ACCOUNTING SYSTEMS

34

Control objective	Assurance provided	No assurance provided
Wages are only paid to genuine employees.	✓	
The payroll is complete and contains the names of all employees.		✓

35

Control objective	Assurance provided	No assurance provided
Obsolete inventory is identified on a timely basis.	✓	
Inventory is valued correctly at the lower of cost and net realisable value.		✓

36

	Strength	Weakness
(a) The manual payroll is processed weekly by Alison who is also responsible for updating employee details such as the addition and deletion of employees and any changes to wage rates.		✓
(b) The Managing Director insists on reviewing a full payroll listing to authorise before he signs the cheque to withdraw the funds from the bank to pay the staff.	✓	
(c) All timesheets, including overtime, are authorised and signed by line managers prior to be sent to the payroll department.	✓	

37

	Strength	Weakness
(a) Customer credit limits are not subject to a regular review and if an urgent order is placed this is despatched without reference to current outstanding credit.		✓
(b) New customers can only obtain goods up to a set order limit and new orders are not despatched until the account is cleared for a period of two months until a credit history is established.	✓	
(c) Sales orders are matched to Goods Despatch Notes and sales invoices. Sales orders are regularly reviewed to identify any unmatched orders.	✓	

38

	Strength	Weakness
(a) The purchasing manager is responsible for all of the stages involved in the purchasing and verifying of goods.		✓
(b) Any changes to staff salaries are notified in writing from the relevant manager to the payroll manager.	✓	
(c) Goods are despatched with no checks taking place on their condition, quantity or completeness.		✓

39

	Strength	Weakness
(a) The computerised payroll is processed weekly by Larissa who is also responsible for amending the standing data details such as the addition of new employees and changes to wage rates.		✓
(b) The Managing Director, Adam, reviews the BACs listing of net pay details per employee and signs the listing before authorising the assistant accountant, Marie, to transmit the details to the company's bank.	✓	

40

	Strength	Weakness
(a) Any discounts from standard selling prices that the sales team would like to offer clients must be approved first by Leo Lemon, the Sales Director.	✓	
(b) Credit notes are not part of the sales system and are raised manually on a word processor by any of the sales administrators.		✓

RISKS AND CONTROLS

41 (a) Paying for goods not received.

(b) Purchasing unnecessary goods.

42 (a) Customers receiving goods that they cannot pay for.

(b) Customers exceeding credit terms set.

43 (a) Staff paid for hours not worked.

(b) Inaccurate wage rates and deductions.

44 (a) Paying for goods not received.

(b) Theft of inventory.

45 (a) Changing people's salaries or diverting money in to a different bank account.

(b) Paying for overtime that was never worked.

VERIFICATION TECHNIQUES

46

Procedure	Test of control	Test of detail	Analytical procedure
Developing an expectation of payroll costs by taking into account last year's payroll figure, annual pay rises and starters and leavers.			✓
Reviewing purchase orders to see if they have been approved by a relevant member of staff.	✓		
Recalculating PAYE and NIC costs for payroll.		✓	
Calculating receivables and payables days and comparing to the prior year.			✓
Reviewing bank reconciliations to ensure they have been prepared and reviewed by an appropriate person.	✓		

47

		Accuracy	Classification	Existence
(a)	Receivables circularisation letter			✓
(b)	After date receipts			✓
(c)	Description of goods		✓	

48

		Valuation	Completeness	Existence
(a)	The auditor seeks assurance that the asset or liability is recorded at the correct value.	✓		
(b)	A full inventory check is performed with the auditor verifying inventory sheets to inventory on shelves.			✓

49

		Accuracy	Classification	Cut-off	Existence
(a)	Date of the invoice.			✓	
(b)	Description of the item purchased.		✓		
(c)	Monetary amount.	✓			

50

	Rights and obligations	Cut-off	Valuation	Classification
(a) Addressee of the invoice.	✓			
(b) Date of the goods received note.		✓		
(c) Description of the item.				✓

COMPUTER-ASSISTED AUDIT TECHNIQUES

51

	Test data	Audit software
(a) The stratification of data to perform full audit testing.		✓
(b) Input of data with false dates to check the system identifies incorrect data for the period.	✓	
(c) The identification of a missing sequence in source documents.		✓

52

	Test data	Audit software
(a) To test that timesheets are not input for non-existent employees.	✓	
(b) To carry out statistical analysis of data within the population.		✓
(c) To check the accuracy of calculations within a spreadsheet.		✓

53

	Test data	Audit software
(a) The auditor enters fictitious data into the computer system and carries out checks that the application controls the system should run have operated as expected.	✓	
(b) The technique is used to examine the client's accounting data including identifying trends and producing aged analysis.		✓
(c) The auditor will look to highlight suspicious items according to pre-determined search criteria.		✓

54

	Test data	Audit software
(a) Comparison of the cost and net realisable value of inventory items to determine the lower value.		✓
(b) Input of data with false inventory code numbers to check that the system rejects such data.	✓	
(c) Extraction of inventory balances over £5,000 in order to carry out further testing.		✓

55

	Test data	Audit software
(a) Calculating a statistically significant sample size for testing the receivables population.		✓
(b) Inputting a credit card into an e-commerce sales system which has gone beyond its expiry date.	✓	
(c) Attempting to assign a VAT rate of greater than 20% to a sales transaction.	✓	

SAMPLING

56 (a) A sampling approach whereby items are chosen in a sequential order. **Block sampling**

(b) A sampling approach whereby items are selected with a constant interval between selections. **Systematic sampling**

(c) The risk that the auditor misinterprets the audit evidence obtained. **Non-sampling risk**

57

	Increase	Decrease	No effect
Being able to test very easily 90% of the sales invoices by way of a proof in total.		✓	
Internal controls are found to be weak and not operating effectively.	✓		
The audit client requesting that the auditor reduces the amount of testing.			✓

TESTS OF CONTROL AND SUBSTANTIVE PROCEDURES

58

	Tests of controls and substantive procedures	Substantive procedures only, with no tests of controls
The audited entity was only set up a year ago, and there is only one member of staff in the accounting department.		✓
There is no segregation of duties within the accounting department of the client.		✓
The client has an internal audit department which reviews controls throughout the year.	✓	

59

	Tests of controls and substantive procedures	Substantive procedures only, with no tests of controls
The entity has a strong control environment.	✓	
A large fraud has been identified which came about due to the collusion of several members of staff.		✓
A new accounting package was introduced at the beginning of the year and there have been significant operational deficiencies with the new system.		✓

60

		Test of control	Substantive procedure
(a)	The distribution and reviewing of receivables circularisation letters.		✓
(b)	Reviewing credit control procedures for recoverability of receivables.	✓	
(c)	Reconcile a sample of debit entries recorded in the ledger and agree to the purchase day book.		✓

61

	Test of control	Substantive procedure
(a) Perform tests on the supplier statement reconciliation process to confirm the completeness of payables.		✓
(b) To carry out checks on the accuracy of recording invoices for prices, discounts, VAT calculation and totals.		✓
(c) To verify that a transaction or event took place which pertains to the entity during the relevant period.		✓

62

	Test of control	Substantive procedure
(a) Comparison of the current year's revenue figure with the previous year's figure.		✓
(b) Observation of the despatch procedures in respect of goods leaving an entity's warehouse.	✓	
(c) Vouching of an addition to non-current assets to the supplier's invoice.		✓

ACCOUNT BALANCES AND ASSOCIATED RISKS

63

	Understated	Overstated
(a) The results show that compared to the previous year trade receivables has increased by 30% and revenue has increased by 9%.		✓
(b) The results show that compared to the previous year trade payables has decreased by 15% and purchases have decreased by 10%.	✓	

64

	Understated	Overstated
(a) The results show that compared to the previous year trade receivables has increased by 20% and revenue has increased by 5%.		✓
(b) The results show that compared to the previous year trade payables has decreased by 10% and purchases have decreased by 7%.	✓	

AUDIT RISK

65

	Yes	No
Inherent risk	✓	
Control risk	✓	
Identity risk		✓
Detection risk	✓	

66 (a) **Control risk** is the risk that a client's internal controls have not detected a material misstatement.

(b) **Detection risk** is the risk that the auditor's procedures do not detect a material misstatement in the financial statements.

(c) **Audit risk** is the risk of the auditor issuing an incorrect audit opinion.

(d) **Inherent risk** is the risk of there being a material misstatement in the financial statements due to the nature of the client.

67

	Increase	Decrease
(a) Sales invoices are only raised for goods that have been dispatched.		✓
(b) No initial credit checks are made on new customers to gauge their creditworthiness.	✓	
(c) All customer receipts are correctly recorded.		✓

68

	Increase	Decrease
(a) Due to cost saving measures, there is less segregation of duties amongst the payroll staff.		✓
(b) The entity has recently introduced a new cash handling procedure with complete procedure notes distributed to all staff.	✓	
(c) Management regularly review budgets and compare to forecasts to analyse the company's performance.	✓	

69

	True	False
(a) External auditors are able to control inherent risk and control risk so as to reduce audit risk to an acceptably low level.		✓
(b) External auditors are able to control detection risk so as to reduce audit risk to an acceptably low level.	✓	

70

		Increase	Decrease	No effect
(a)	The entity is committed to employing personnel with appropriate accounting and financial reporting skills.		✓	
(b)	The entity is to be sold and the purchase consideration will be determined as a multiple of reported profit.	✓		
(c)	The entity's management does not intend to remedy deficiencies in internal controls identified by the external auditor.	✓		

MATERIALITY

71

		True	False
(a)	As part of the audit planning, the auditor will determine the maximum amount of errors he is willing to accept and still be satisfied that the financial statements show a true and fair view.	✓	
(b)	Materiality is equally important to the auditor when expressing an opinion and the management when reviewing the financial statements.		✓

72

		True	False
(a)	A material error in the financial statements may be described as the relative significance or importance of a particular matter in the context of the financial statements.	✓	
(b)	A material error in the financial statements may be described as a lack of robust written processes and procedures in place to record each stage of a transaction.		✓

73

		True	False
(a)	Materiality is not capable of general mathematical definition as it has both qualitative and quantitative aspects.	✓	
(b)	The auditor will consider a relatively small error in a month end procedure an indication of a potential material misstatement if that error is repeated each month.	✓	

74

		True	False
(a)	When determining materiality, the auditor just looks at the size of an item in comparison to the profit of the client.		✓
(b)	Auditing standards specify what percentage of profit would make an item material.		✓

75

		True	False
(a)	Performance materiality is set a level above materiality as it only relates to the financial statements as a whole.		✓
(b)	The idea behind performance materiality is to reduce to an acceptably low level the probability that the aggregate uncorrected and undetected misstatements exceed materiality for the financial statements as a whole.	✓	

76

		True	False
(a)	Performance materiality should be set at a level below the level of materiality for the financial statements as a whole.	✓	
(b)	Once established, performance materiality must not be changed as the audit progresses.		✓

77

		True	False
(a)	Performance materiality is always a given percentage of overall materiality.		✓
(b)	All errors found, in excess of performance materiality, must be amended by the client in order to avoid the audit report being qualified.		✓

INFORMATION AND RECOMMENDATIONS FOR THE AUDIT PLAN

78   Multiple sites

- The external auditor may not be able to visit all of the sites. They will have to establish which ones to visit, and then visit the others on a rotational basis.

Wages

- Casual workers are paid cash in hand which increases the risk of misappropriation of cash.

- PAYE/NIC may not be calculated correctly.

Cash sales

- Significant number of cash sales which increases the risk of misappropriation of cash.

- Risk of understatement of sales.

- No reconciliations of tills

  - Cash could be misappropriated.

  - Sales could be understated.

  - Lack of control from Head Office.

- Purchases

  - There is no check of invoices to goods actually received.

  - Company may pay for goods not received or good than were of low quality.

79 Receivables

- Customers are invoiced after installation which could cause issues collecting money.

- Risk of irrecoverable receivables.

Revenue recognition

- The revenue for the service support contracts should be spread over the period to which the contract relates. This could result in overstatement of revenue if not done correctly.

- Deferred income may be misstated on the statement of financial position.

Inventory

- Different types of inventory which could cause issues for valuation purposes.

- Valuation of WIP is notoriously difficult due to the nature and establishing the stage of completion.

Foreign currency transactions

- Risk of inappropriate exchange rates used which can cause errors in purchases, payables and inventory.

Warranty provision

- This is a judgmental area in the financial statements.

- Will need to understand the assumptions underlying the provision.

- How accurate has the provision been in the past?

80 • Going concern risk if company fails to comply with the terms of the loan.

- Misclassification of the loan in the financial statements i.e. split between current and non-current liability.

- Manipulation of financial statements to meet loan covenants.

- Incorrect calculation of interest.

- Failure to record loan and loan repayments.

- Incorrect disclosure of the loan terms and interest.

- Project incorrectly capitalised and depreciated.

81
- Incorrect classification of the lorries within non-current assets.
- Incorrect classification of the finance agreement within liabilities i.e. split between current and non-current liability.
- Incorrect calculation of the finance liability.
- Inappropriate depreciation policy.
- Incorrect calculation of depreciation.
- Inaccurate cost figures used.
- Incorrect calculation of interest on the loan.
- Incorrect disclosure of the loan terms and interest.
- Recording purchase in wrong period.
- Failure to record the new assets at all.
- Failure to record loan repayments.

82
- Statutory fines and penalties which would need to be provided for in the financial statements.
- Provisions may be omitted or understated in the financial statements.
- Increased insurance premiums which could have an adverse effect on cash flow which could lead to going concern issues.
- Loss of reputation may lead to forced closure which could lead to going concern issues and may mean the financial statements need to be prepared on the break up basis.

VERIFICATION OF ITEMS IN THE FINANCIAL STATEMENTS

83
- Obtain a breakdown of the work in progress balance, cast it and ensure the total agrees to the figure in the financial statements.
- Test a sample of entries for materials to purchase invoices.
- Complete weekly reconciliations of cash sales to receivables.
- Trace a sample of invoices to costing records.
- Trace a sample of timesheet/payroll details to the costing records.
- Carry out analytical procedures to determine overall performance.
- Discuss with management process for determining stage of completion and determine if reasonable.
- If applicable, discuss the method of calculating the overhead absorption rate and re-calculate to ensure reasonable.

84
- Obtain a breakdown of non-current assets, cast it and ensure the total agrees to the figure in the financial statements.

- Select a sample of items from the asset register and then physically inspect them to confirm existence.

- Select a sample of visible assets and inspect the relevant entry in the asset register to confirm the latter is complete.

- Select a sample of items from the register and inspect their source ownership documents (such as invoices, lease agreements) to confirm the terms of acquisition and, hence, ownership.

- Add up all items in the asset register to confirm the documents' mathematical accuracy.

- Recalculate a sample of depreciation charges to confirm the mathematical accuracy of the register.

- Compare the totals on the register with that of the nominal ledger to confirm the accuracy of financial records/ledgers.

- Review P&L accounts such as repairs and renewals to ensure all assets have been capitalised.

85
- Obtain a breakdown of receivables, cast it and ensure the total agrees to the figure in the financial statements.

- Stratify the population in order to conduct sample testing.

- Perform a direct confirmation of a sample of receivables.

- Obtain aged receivables analysis and cast for accuracy.

- Review reconciliation from receivables ledger control account to receivables ledger.

- Perform after date cash test on a sample of receivables.

- Calculate receivables days and compare with prior year.

- Compare ageing of receivables with prior year.

- Review aged receivables list for any overdue debts and discuss with Credit Controller.

- Review above debts for inclusion in specific bad debt provision.

- Enquire as to methodology behind any general bad debt provision.

- Recalculate general bad debt provision based on client's methodology.

- Agree receivables figure to draft FS.

- Agree ageing of a sample of specific receivables by agreeing to invoices.

- Review receivables ledger for any credit balances.

AUDIT DOCUMENTATION

86

Working paper	Reason for preparation
Independence questionnaire completed by each member of the audit team.	Compliance with independence and ethical requirements
Copies of cash flow and profit forecasts and post year-end management accounts.	Assess the going concern status
Details of the review of assets in the factory whilst attending the inventory count.	Supporting valuation of assets

87

		True	False
(a)	Working papers must only be prepared in electronic form to ensure confidentiality and security.		✓
(b)	There are two main types of file for audit working papers; the permanent audit file and the current audit file.	✓	
(c)	The date of the working papers and the name of the person preparing the file should be clearly stated on all documents.	✓	

88

		True	False
(a)	The audit working papers are prepared and collated during the audit and should be retained in connection with the performance of the audit.	✓	
(b)	The permanent audit file should not contain any copies of statutory or legal regulations or papers.		✓
(c)	The current audit file should include schedules showing the results of audit tests carried out.	✓	

89

		True	False
(a)	The auditor's working papers provide adequate evidence of the work that has been carried out and the conclusions reached contain sufficient appropriate audit evidence to support the conclusions made.	✓	
(b)	The auditor will rely on a designated staff member from the client's workforce to assist in the compilation of the current audit file.		✓
(c)	The permanent audit files contain information of continuing importance to the audit such as board minutes of relevance, previous years' signed accounts analytical reviews and engagement letters.	✓	

90

		True	False
(a)	Working papers are prepared by the external auditor because there is a legal requirement to do so.		✓
(b)	The objective of working papers is to provide evidence that the audit was planned and performed in accordance with International Standards on Auditing.	✓	
(c)	Working papers should contain the name of who performed the audit work and the date it was performed.	✓	

91

		True	False
(a)	The detailed content of each type of audit working paper is strictly detailed in the ISAs.		✓
(b)	The primary objective of working papers is to prove to the audit partner that the work was done.		✓
(c)	Working papers should clearly state which year-end they pertain to and show evidence that they have been reviewed.	✓	

IDENTIFY MATTERS OF AN UNUSUAL NATURE

92

No further action	Refer to supervisor
	✓

93

No further action	Refer to supervisor
	✓

94

No further action	Refer to supervisor
	✓

95

No further action	Refer to supervisor
✓	

96

No further action	Refer to supervisor
✓	

97

No further action	Refer to supervisor
	✓

98

No further action	Refer to supervisor
✓	

99

No further action	Refer to supervisor
✓	

DRAFT REPORTS AND RECOMMENDATIONS

100 **(a)** **Consequences**

- Equipment recorded in the register may not exist or may have been stolen.

- Acquisitions or disposals may not be recorded.

- Equipment may be fully written down but still in use.

- Equipment may be impaired and consequently overvalued.

- Depreciation charges on the equipment may be inappropriate.

(b) **Recommendations**

- Periodic reconciliation of:

  – physical equipment to register to ensure completeness of recording

  – entries in the register to physical equipment to ensure existence and in good condition.

- Reconciliation to be performed independent of custodian.

- Differences to be reported and investigated.

- Monitoring of procedures to ensure checks undertaken.

101 **(a)** **Consequences**

- Relevant price may not be the most up to date.

- Sales ledger clerk may update the price incorrectly.

- Sales ledger clerk may manipulate the sales price on the master file fraudulently.

- Sales invoices may be raised incorrectly due to incorrect sales price being used.

(b) **Recommendations**

- Sales director should review and authorise all sales price updates.

- Sales director should inform the sales ledger clerk of updated with written confirmation to ensure an audit trail.

- Reconciliation to be performed between a sample of sales invoices with the sales price on the master file.

102 **(a)** **Consequences**

- Goods may be broken/damaged on arrival and we cannot later claim from the supplier.

- We may accept goods which were not as ordered, or not ordered at all.

- The wrong person may be emailed and the goods may not be claimed.

- The person who ordered the goods may not get the email and may re-order the goods thinking they have not arrived.

- The goods could be stolen or damaged while in the warehouse waiting to be collected.

(b) **Recommendations**

- A copy of the purchase order should be sent to the warehouse in preparation for the goods arriving.

- The copy order should clearly state who should be contacted when the goods arrive.

- The warehouse staff should check the quality of the goods when they arrive.

- The warehouse staff should agree the content of the goods to the details on the order.

- The warehouse staff should complete a Goods Received Note (GRN) detailing the goods received and evidencing that they have performed the above checks.

- The goods received notes should be sequentially numbered.

- A copy of the GRN should be sent to the person who placed the order to say the good are to be collected.

- When they come to the warehouse to collect the goods, they should sign the warehouse copy of the GRN to evidence collection.

- The warehouse should keep a copy of the completed GRN with their copy of the order.

AUDIT REPORTS

103

(a)   In our opinion:

The financial statements give a true and fair view, in accordance with UK Generally Accepted Accounting Practice, of the state of the company's affairs as at 31 March 2008 and of its profit for the year then ended.

The financial statements have been properly prepared in accordance with the Companies Act 2006; and the information given in the Directors' Report is consistent with the financial statements.

(b)   Extract:

I planned my audit so as to obtain all the information and explanations which I considered necessary in order to provide me with sufficient evidence to give reasonable assurance that the financial statements are free from material misstatements. In forming my opinion I also evaluated the overall adequacy of the presentation of information in the financial statements. However, the evidence available to me was limited by the fundamental uncertainties that meant I was unable to form an opinion on the financial statements. In the circumstances we are unable to form an audit opinion.

	Qualified opinion	Unmodified opinion	Disclaimer of opinion
(a)		✓	
(b)			✓

104   A

The auditor would qualify their opinion on the grounds of insufficient evidence with regard to a matter that could be material but not pervasive.

105

	Modified	Not modified
(a) Ash Co capitalised costs of £150,000 in respect of repairs and maintenance and included these costs in non-current assets. The amount capitalised represents 30% of Ash Co's profit before tax. The directors refuse to make any adjustments in respect of this matter.	✓	
(b) There is a significant uncertainty about Medlar Co's ability to continue as a going concern. The directors of Medlar Co have prepared the financial statements on a going concern basis and have fully disclosed the uncertainty in the notes to the financial statements.		✓

106

	Modified	Not modified
(a) There is a claim against Santa Co which is waiting to go to court. The opinion of the Directors is that they are unlikely to have to pay any damages. The auditor agrees with this judgement. The Directors have made a full disclosure of this situation in the accounts. Although potentially material, the damages would not have a significant impact on the company.		✓
(b) Elves Co has a receivable which owes the company £125,000. No payments have been made on this debt for 6 months. This represents 20% of the overall receivables figure, 2% of revenue and 15% of profit for the year. The client refuses to provide for this amount as they believe that once the new management team at the client are settled in, regular payments will start to be made.	✓	

107 For each of the following situations which have arisen in Alba Co, select the impact on the auditor's report on the financial statements.

	Adverse opinion	Unmodified opinion with a Material Uncertainty Related to Going Concern section included in the audit report	Unmodified opinion with an Emphasis of Matter paragraph
(a) The directors of Alba Co have produced a cash flow forecast which shows a significantly worsening position over the coming 12 months. The auditors have been informed that Alba's bankers will not make a decision on the renewal of the overdraft facility until after the auditor's report is completed. The directors have agreed to include some going concern disclosures. The auditor believes the disclosures made by the directors are adequate.		✓	
(b) In relation to the above scenario, the auditor believes the basis of preparation of the financial statements is incorrect.	✓		

Section 3

MOCK ASSESSMENT QUESTIONS

TASK 1.1

(2 marks)

Identify the level of assurance provided by the following extracts.

	Extract	Reasonable assurance	Limited assurance
1	In our opinion, the financial statements give a true and fair view of the state of the company's affairs as at 31 December X8 and of its profit for the year then ended.		
2	Nothing has come to our attention that indicates the internal control systems are not operating effectively.		

TASK 1.2

(3 marks)

Below are three statements regarding an external audit of financial statements conducted under International Standards on Auditing (ISAs).

Identify whether each statement is true or false.

	Statement	True	False
1	The external auditor is responsible for expressing an opinion on whether the financial statements show a true and fair view.		
2	The external auditor is responsible for detecting fraud.		
3	The amounts in the financial statements are presented precisely.		

TASK 1.3

(3 marks)

Complete the following statements relating to the external auditor's liability.

Pick list
Third parties
Professional indemnity insurance
Shareholders
Liability cap

1   This is compulsory for all accountants who have a practising certificate. _____

2   The inclusion of a statement disclaiming liability in the audit report may reduce the risk of claims from _____.

TASK 1.4 (4 marks)

(a)   **For each of the following descriptions, identify the concept it represents.**

   1   To avoid any action that discredits the profession. _____

   2   Not to allow bias or conflict of interest when making professional or business decisions. _____

   Select from: Independence, Professional competence and due care, Objectivity, Professional behaviour

(b)   **Which one of the following situations is likely to give rise to a self-interest threat?**

The engagement partner has been in place for a number of years.	
Assisting management with the selection of a new accounting package.	
Owning shares in the client company.	

TASK 1.5 (2 marks)

Below are two statements regarding potential safeguards to be applied to protect an external auditor's independence and objectivity.

Identify whether each statement below is true or false.

	Statement	True	False
1	The external auditor should review the engagement if the level of regular fees exceed 15% of practice income for a listed client.		
2	If a senior member of staff leaves to join an audit client, an independent partner should review their recent work on that client.		

TASK 1.6 (3 marks)

There are certain circumstances in which an external auditor must or may disclose confidential information relating to a client. Some circumstances require the client's permission, whilst others do not.

Identify whether each of the following circumstances requires the external auditor to obtain the client's permission in order to disclose the information.

	Requires the client's permission	Does NOT require the client's permission
The provision of evidence whilst the auditor is defending themselves in court.		
The external auditor suspects that the client is involved in money laundering.		
A request for information regarding the client's financial statements from the client's solicitor.		

TASK 1.7   (3 marks)

When evaluating internal controls at an audit client, the external auditor needs to understand a number of technical terms.

For each of the descriptions below, identify the technical term to which it relates.

- The general attitude of management about the importance of control. _____

- The allocation of different tasks within a system to different personnel. _____

- This function can be performed in house or can be outsourced. _____

Select from: Collusion, External audit, Risk assessment process, Internal audit, Segregation of duties, Control environment

TASK 1.8   (3 marks)

Accounting systems have control procedures to mitigate the risk that a control objective is not met.

Identify whether each element below is a control objective, risk or control procedure.

		Objective	Risk	Procedure
1	Employees are paid for work they have not performed.			
2	To ensure income tax and national insurance deductions are paid in a timely fashion.			
3	Comparison of names on the weekly payroll summary with names of current staff in human resources records.			

TASK 1.9   (5 marks)

The internal control checklist for Nicely Co indicates that all purchase orders are authorised by the Head of Procurement, with any orders over £10,000 being authorised by one of the Directors.

(a)   Identify whether or not this would provide assurance on each of the following control objectives.

		Assurance provided	No assurance provided
1	Only high quality goods are accepted into the business.		
2	All purchases are valid business expenses.		

(b) Identify whether each of the following procedures within a purchases system is a strength or a deficiency.

		Strength	Deficiency
1	The Purchasing Manager is responsible for ordering goods, posting the inventory movement and posting the purchase invoice to the nominal ledger.		
2	The warehouse supervisor checks the quality of goods before he signs to accept the delivery.		
3	Purchase orders are matched to Goods Received Notes and orders are reviewed regularly to check for any unmatched ones.		

TASK 1.10 (4 marks)

An entity uses internal control procedures to mitigate the risks to which it is exposed.

Match each internal control procedure to the risk it mitigates.

Internal control procedure		Risk mitigated
1	The Finance Director reviews purchase invoices before signing cheques.	
2	Regular review of inventory items which haven't been sold for 3 months.	

Select from: Accepting goods of poor quality, Obsolete inventory, Paying for non-business related goods, Theft of inventory

TASK 1.11 (4 marks)

(a) Auditors use tests of control and substantive procedures to gather audit evidence.

For each of the procedures listed below, select whether it is a test of control or a substantive procedure.

		Test of control	Substantive procedure
1	Inspection of a sample of month end salary payment schedules to ensure they have been signed by an appropriate level of management prior to being processed.		
2	Inspection of a purchase invoice and comparison of the total price on it to the amount recorded in the purchase ledger.		
3	Inspection of a tangible, non-current vehicle asset to identify any signs of damage.		

(b) **In respect of the procedures below, select the assertion for which assurance is being sought.**

		Completeness	Existence	Valuation	Rights
1	Selecting a sample of inventory items off the inventory listing from the accounting system and comparing the quantities to physical amounts in the warehouse.				
2	Selecting a sample of physical inventory items in the warehouse and comparing the quantities counted to the inventory listing from the accounting system.				
3	Physically inspecting inventory items for evidence of damage or ageing.				

TASK 1.12   (2 marks)

Two types of computer assisted audit techniques (CAATs) are test data and audit software.

Identify for each of the procedures listed below, the type of CAAT that would be used to perform that procedure.

	Procedure	Test data	Audit software
1	Extraction of post year-end sales and purchases information in relation to long term contracts that are being tested.		
2	Input of a sales order for a customer who has exceeded their credit limit to see if the system flags the error.		

TASK 1.13   (4 marks)

(a) When using sampling techniques in auditing, the external auditor needs to understand a number of technical terms.

Identify the technical term for each of the descriptions below.

- A sampling approach whereby all items in the population have an equal chance of selection._____

- A sampling approach whereby items are selected with no particular reasoning._____

- The risk that the auditor misinterprets the audit evidence._____

Select from: Stratification, Block sampling, Random sampling, Systematic sampling, Haphazard sampling, Sampling risk, Non-sampling risk

(b)   When selecting items in order to perform tests of detail, the external auditor has to consider a number of factors.

Identify whether the following factor will result in an increase in sample size, a decrease in sample size or have a negligible effect on sample size for substantive testing.

The internal controls of an audit client are found to be ineffective and there are many instances throughout the year of management override.

TASK 1.14 (3 marks)

The external auditor may adopt an audit approach which involves undertaking either:

- tests of controls and substantive procedures, or

- substantive procedures only, with no tests of controls.

Identify the most likely approach to be adopted by the external auditor in each of the following circumstances.

		Tests of control and substantive procedures	Substantive procedures only with no tests of controls
1	The Finance Director left last year and was not replaced and all members of the Finance department are relatively new, having only been in place for a few months.		
2	The audit client outsources the internal audit function, who visit three times per year and review all systems. Recommendations are always implemented.		
3	There is segregation of duties within the Finance department of the audit client.		

TASK 1.15 (2 marks)

You are responsible for testing that trade payables are fairly stated in the financial statements of an audit client.

Identify whether the following audit procedure would test for understatement or overstatement of trade payables.

Reviewing the unpaid invoices file and tracing invoices to ledgers.

TASK 1.16 (10 marks)

(a) Audit risk is the product of inherent risk, control risk and detection risk. The external auditor assesses inherent risk and control risk to determine the audit approach.

Identify whether each of the following statements in respect of audit risk and its components is true or false.

		True	False
1	Detection risk is the only element of audit risk that the auditor can control.		
2	Control risk is the risk that the auditor assesses controls as strong when in fact they are not operating effectively.		

(b) **Identify whether each of the following factors is likely to lead to the auditor assessing control risk as higher or lower.**

		Control risk higher	Control risk lower
1	Half way through the year your client replaced their sales and purchases accounting system. At the year-end half the accounts staff have received training by the system provider.		
2	You are about to start planning a client's audit. You have come across a note on last year's working papers that there is some suspicion of managerial control override and possible fraud, although there is no proof of this.		
3	Your client has stopped performing sales and purchases reconciliations as they no longer see the value in them.		

(c) **Identify whether or not each of the following actions will increase or decrease detection risk.**

		Increase	Decrease
1	The Finance Director would like the audit completed two months after the year end so that he can go on an extended holiday during the Easter school holidays.		
2	Following a review of audit risk, the auditor has decided to substantially increase sample sizes.		
3	The use of a solicitor to confirm the disclosure of a contingent liability is appropriate.		

(d) The external auditor is required to undertake analytical procedures as part of the planning to identify the risk of misstatement in the financial statements.

The gross profit margin of Green Grass Co, a manufacturing company, has increased in comparison to the prior year.

Which one of the following may provide a plausible explanation for the increase in Green Grass Co's gross profit margin?

_____

Select from: Understatement of closing work in progress, Unfavourable exchange rate movements on goods purchased from overseas, Overstatement of closing work in progress, A large increase in the warranty provision

TASK 1.17

(3 marks)

Identify whether each of the following statements is true or false in respect of materiality.

		True	False
1	International Standards on Auditing specify clearly how to calculate materiality.		
2	Failure by the audit client to provide for an irrecoverable receivable that represents 12% of profit before tax would generally be considered to be material but not pervasive.		
3	Performance materiality is always set at a level higher than normal materiality.		

TASK 1.18 (10 marks)

During the financial year under review, your audit client disposed of an old warehouse and purchased a new warehouse. The purchase price of the warehouse was £1.5 million and there were associated agent's fees of £20,000. The company also incurred an additional £50,000 performing repairs to the property so that it could be brought into working order. The warehouse was occupied by the client 3 months before the year end.

Once operational, a further £15,000 costs were incurred to correct a fault; the wrong sort of wiring was installed by your client when bringing the asset into working condition.

The company adopts the revaluation policy for its land and buildings. A revaluation was not deemed necessary at the year-end due to the recent purchase.

Identify and explain the audit risks relating to the acquisition and disposal of the warehouse.

TASK 1.19

(10 marks)

During the audit of a client you read a press release that indicates that 'Toxchem', a product which forms a major part of your client's sales, contains a chemical that has been identified as being potentially dangerous to those who handle it. An official government working party has been set up to review the situation.

Set out in a manner suitable for inclusion in the audit plan, the audit procedures to be undertaken in order to ensure that adequate provisions and contingent liabilities have been created for potential legal claims with regard to this matter.

TASK 1.20 (3 marks)

Audit documentation serves a number of purposes.

Identify the purpose of each of the working papers in the table below by dragging the appropriate reason for preparation next to each working paper.

Working paper		Reason for preparation
1	Copies of profit and cash flow forecasts.	
2	Responses from receivables circularisation.	
3	Review of post year-end sales prices for a sample of inventory lines.	

Select from: Support valuation of inventory, Assess going concern status, Assess accuracy of receivables, Assess the quantity of inventory, Assess existence of receivables, Assess future profitability.

TASK 1.21 (3 marks)

During the audit of Blue Chip Co, the audit junior identified three matters which he considered to be unusual.

Identify whether each of the matters listed below should be referred to the audit supervisor.

Matter		Refer to supervisor	Do not refer to supervisor
1	You have just performed a reconciliation of payroll records to human resources records and you have identified that there is an employee on the payroll who left the company three months prior to the year-end. Their salary is still being processed at the end of each month. All payroll amounts are processed and authorised by the Financial Controller on a monthly basis.		
2	The writing down of one line of inventory as its expiry date is 3 weeks after the year-end.		
3	It was discovered that significant sales were made to a company controlled by the Managing Director. The Managing Director has told the audit junior this is not significant and asked him not to mention it further.		

TASK 1.22 (10 marks)

During the audit of Geek Co, a manufacturer of calculators, it was discovered that although the company raises a three part despatch note upon despatch of orders from the warehouse the document is assigned a random code, made up by the stores team. Also, only one person picks and packs the goods ready for despatch.

Prepare extracts, suitable for inclusion in a report to management of Geek Co, which set out

(i) the possible consequences; and

(ii) the recommendations that you would make in respect of this matter.

TASK 1.23 (4 marks)

For each of the following situations, which have arisen in two unrelated audit clients, select whether or not the audit opinion on the financial statements would be modified.

		Modified	Not modified
1	One of your audit clients, Pink Co, has old inventory valued at £20,000 remaining on their statement of financial position. Your audit evidence appears to suggest that in the current climate the maximum the items could be sold for is £7,500. The required impairment would represent approximately 2% of profits.		
2	One of your clients, Blue Co, outsourced credit control to an external agency during the year. All the receivables information is now managed by the external agency. Despite your requests the external agency has refused you access to their books and records. Receivables represent 10% of Blue's total assets.		

Section 4

MOCK ASSESSMENT ANSWERS

TASK 1.1

Extract		Reasonable assurance	Limited assurance
1	In our opinion, the financial statements give a true and fair view of the state of the company's affairs as at 31 December X8 and of its profit for the year then ended.	✓	
2	Nothing has come to our attention that indicates the internal control systems are not operating effectively.		✓

TASK 1.2

Statement		True	False
1	The external auditor is responsible for expressing an opinion on whether the financial statements show a true and fair view.	✓	
2	The external auditor is responsible for detecting fraud.		✓
3	The amounts in the financial statements are presented precisely.		✓

TASK 1.3

1   Professional indemnity insurance

2   Third parties

TASK 1.4

(a)   1   Professional behaviour

2   Objectivity

(b)

The engagement partner has been in place for a number of years.	
Assisting management with the selection of a new accounting package.	
Owning shares in the client company.	✓

TASK 1.5

Statement		True	False
1	The external auditor should review the engagement if the level of regular fees exceed 15% of practice income for a listed client.		✓
2	If a senior member of staff leaves to join an audit client, an independent partner should review their recent work on that client.	✓	

TASK 1.6

	Requires the client's permission	Does NOT require the client's permission
The provision of evidence whilst the auditor is defending themselves in court.		✓
The external auditor suspects that the client is involved in money laundering.		✓
A request for information regarding the client's financial statements from the client's solicitor.	✓	

TASK 1.7

- Control environment
- Segregation of duties
- Internal audit

TASK 1.8

		Objective	Risk	Procedure
1	Employees are paid for work they have not performed.		✓	
2	To ensure income tax and national insurance deductions are paid in a timely fashion.	✓		
3	Comparison of names on the weekly payroll summary with names of current staff in human resources records.			✓

TASK 1.9

(a)

		Assurance provided	No assurance provided
1	Only high quality goods are accepted into the business.		✓
2	All purchases are valid business expenses.	✓	

(b)

		Strength	Deficiency
1	The Purchasing Manager is responsible for ordering goods, posting the inventory movement and posting the purchase invoice to the nominal ledger.		✓
2	The warehouse supervisor checks the quality of goods before he signs to accept the delivery.	✓	
3	Purchase orders are matched to Goods Received Notes and orders are reviewed regularly to check for any unmatched ones.	✓	

TASK 1.10

Internal control procedure		Risk mitigated
1	The Finance Director reviews purchase invoices before signing cheques.	Paying for non-business related goods
2	Regular review of inventory items which haven't been sold for 3 months.	Obsolete inventory

TASK 1.11

(a)

		Test of control	Substantive procedure
1	Inspection of a sample of month end salary payment schedules to ensure they have been signed by an appropriate level of management prior to being processed.	✓	
2	Inspection of a purchase invoice and comparison of the total price on it to the amount recorded in the purchase ledger.		✓
3	Inspection of a tangible, non-current vehicle asset to identify any signs of damage.		✓

(b)

		Completeness	Existence	Valuation	Rights
1	Selecting a sample of inventory items off the inventory listing from the accounting system and comparing the quantities to physical amounts in the warehouse.		✓		
2	Selecting a sample of physical inventory items in the warehouse and comparing the quantities counted to the inventory listing from the accounting system.	✓			
3	Physically inspecting inventory items for evidence of damage or ageing.			✓	

TASK 1.12

Procedure		Test data	Audit software
1	Extraction of post year-end sales and purchases information in relation to long term contracts that are being tested.		✓
2	Input of a sales order for a customer who has exceeded their credit limit to see if the system flags the error.	✓	

TASK 1.13

(a) • Random sampling

• Haphazard sampling

• Non-sampling risk

(b) Increase in sample size

TASK 1.14

		Tests of control and substantive procedures	Substantive procedures only with no tests of controls
1	The Finance Director left last year and was not replaced and all members of the Finance department are relatively new, having only been in place for a few months.		✓
2	The audit client outsources the internal audit function, who visit three times per year and review all systems. Recommendations are always implemented.	✓	
3	There is segregation of duties within the Finance department of the audit client.	✓	

TASK 1.15

Understatement

TASK 1.16

(a)

		True	False
1	Detection risk is the only element of audit risk that the auditor can control.	✓	
2	Control risk is the risk that the auditor assesses controls as strong when in fact they are not operating effectively.		✓

(b)

		Control risk higher	Control risk lower
1	Half way through the year your client replaced their sales and purchases accounting system. At the year-end half the accounts staff have received training by the system provider.	✓	
2	You are about to start planning a client's audit. You have come across a note on last year's working papers that there is some suspicion of managerial control override and possible fraud, although there is no proof of this.	✓	
3	Your client has stopped performing sales and purchases reconciliations as they no longer see the value in them.	✓	

(c)

		Increase	Decrease
1	The Finance Director would like the audit completed two months after the year end so that he can go on an extended holiday during the Easter school holidays.	✓	
2	Following a review of audit risk, the auditor has decided to substantially increase sample sizes.		✓
3	The use of a solicitor to confirm the disclosure of a contingent liability is appropriate.		✓

(d) Overstatement of closing work in progress

TASK 1.17

		True	False
1	International Standards on Auditing specify clearly how to calculate materiality.		✓
2	Failure by the audit client to provide for an irrecoverable receivable that represents 12% of profit before tax would generally be considered to be material but not pervasive.	✓	
3	Performance materiality is always set at a level higher than normal materiality.		✓

TASK 1.18

- An incorrect cost may be capitalised: this should only include the purchase cost and directly attributable costs (i.e. £1.57 million – the £15k relating to the faulty wiring cannot be capitalised).

- The cost may not be appropriately split between the land and the building component.

- An incorrect depreciation charge may be calculated if the land and building component are not split accurately.

- Further repair costs may be capitalised as part of the asset cost.

- An incorrect depreciation charge may be calculated in the year of acquisition due to not time apportioning the depreciation charge effectively.

- The old warehouse may not be correctly derecognised.

- The profit or loss on disposal of the old warehouse may not be calculated accurately.

- Any previous balance on the revaluation reserve relating to the old warehouse may not have been released through retained earnings.

- Depending on the economic environment, property values could have altered significantly since the purchase, hence a revaluation may be needed.

TASK 1.19

- Inspect the provisions recorded in the financial statements to identify whether any amounts have been provided for the cost of probable legal claims.

- Inspect the financial statements to identify whether any contingent liability disclosures have been made with regard to possible legal claims.

- Enquire of management how they determined the likelihood of any claims following the government review.

- Obtain a written representation confirming that management have considered the likelihood of any claims and have made all appropriate provisions/contingent liability disclosures as necessary.

- Inspect any legal correspondence/correspondence with government health authorities to identify the likely outcome of the government review.

- Consider events after the reporting period with regard to the outcome of the governments review to identify the need for any adjustments to reported provisions/contingencies.

- Seek the advice of a legal expert and form an independent opinion regarding the likelihood of legal claims being made in response to the government review.

- Review board minutes for during the year and after the year-end to identify any further information which could help to determine the level of provision required.

TASK 1.20

Working paper		Reason for preparation
1	Copies of profit and cash flow forecasts.	Assess going concern status
2	Responses from receivables circularisation.	Assess existence of receivables
3	Review of post year-end sales prices for a sample of inventory lines.	Support valuation of inventory

TASK 1.21

	Matter	Refer to supervisor	Do not refer to supervisor
1	You have just performed a reconciliation of payroll records to human resources records and you have identified that there is an employee on the payroll who left the company three months prior to the year-end. Their salary is still being processed at the end of each month. All payroll amounts are processed and authorised by the Financial Controller on a monthly basis.	✓	
2	The writing down of one line of inventory as its expiry date is 3 weeks after the year-end.		✓
3	It was discovered that significant sales were made to a company controlled by the Managing Director. The Managing Director has told the audit junior this is not significant and asked him not to mention it further.	✓	

TASK 1.22

(i) **Possible consequences**

- Missing goods despatched notes may not be identified because there is no easy way to spot missing items.

- The accounts team may not be informed that a sale requires invoicing.

- Income may be lost or, at the very least, this could delay the collecting of cash from the customer.

- Incorrect goods could be sent out to customers.

(ii) **Recommendations**

- Goods despatched notes should be allocated sequentially numbered references.

- Periodically, a member of the accounts team should perform a review of goods despatched notes to ensure that the sequence for documents received by them, and consequently invoiced, is complete.

- Two people should be involved in the picking process, with one person picking and one person checking the goods.

- Goods despatched notes should be signed once the check of goods has taken place.

TASK 1.23

		Modified	Not modified
1	One of your audit clients, Pink Co, has old inventory valued at £20,000 remaining on their statement of financial position. Your audit evidence appears to suggest that in the current climate the maximum the items could be sold for is £7,500. The required impairment would represent approximately 2% of profits.		✓
2	One of your clients, Blue Co, outsourced credit control to an external agency during the year. All the receivables information is now managed by the external agency. Despite your requests the external agency has refused you access to their books and records. Receivables represent 10% of Blue's total assets.	✓	

KAPLAN PUBLISHING